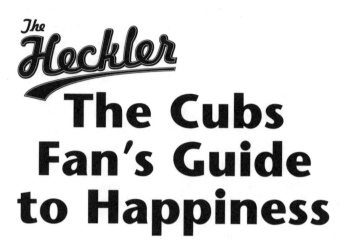

The Heckler
The Cubs Fan's Guide to Happiness

GEORGE ELLIS

TRIUMPH
BOOKS

Library of Congress Cataloging-in-Publication Data

Ellis, George, 1977–
    The Cubs fan's guide to happiness / George Ellis.
       p. cm.
    ISBN: 978-1-57243-936-8
       1. Chicago Cubs (Baseball team)—History. 2. Chicago Cubs (Baseball team)—Humor I. Title.

GV875.C6E45 2007
796.3570977311—dc22

                                                        2006037831

This book is available in quantity at special discounts for your group or organization. For further information, contact:

Triumph Books
542 South Dearborn Street
Suite 750
Chicago, Illinois 60605
(312) 939-3330
Fax (312) 663-3557

Printed in U.S.A.
ISBN: 978-1-57243-936-8
Design by Patricia Frey
All photos courtesy of AP/Wide World Photos unless otherwise indicated
Illustrations by Vito Sabsay

Contents

Acknowledgments

This book would not have been possible without the help of so many people, none of whom are named Ozzie Guillen. First I'd like to recognize Brad Zibung and everyone that makes *The Heckler* the finest satirical sports publication in the world, or at least in Chicago. Someday our little paper will buy the *Tribune* and turn the Cubs into winners.

Thanks to talented illustrator Vito Sabsay for providing drawings I could never do on my own, no matter how hard I tried. His illustrations bring this book to life, which is good, because nobody wants to buy a dead book, especially one written about the Cubs.

Thanks to Brian Summerfield, who helped research and write much of the 100 Frustrations list. Despite being a White Sox fan, Brian's writing is surprisingly coherent and engaging.

Thanks to Alec MacDonald and Danielle Egan-Miller for helping get this project off the ground and into the hands of the people at Triumph Books.

Thanks to Drew Wehrle, whose idea and research gave birth to the Goin' Deep sidebars, ensuring this book's success in academic circles.

Thanks to my wife for putting up with my late-night writing sessions, to my mom for being a Cubs fan, and to my dad (even though he's a Sox fan) for not forcing me to root for the South Siders.

Last but not least, there are some people and entities I would specifically *not* like to thank: the 1969 New York Mets, Steve Garvey, Ronnie Woo Woo, Dennis FitzSimons, and A.J. Pierzynski.

Introduction

The brain of the average Cubs fan works like the brain of the average human, except for one little detail: it has no concept of reality.

Normal people buy lottery tickets thinking they might get lucky. Cubs fans buy lottery tickets expecting to win because they've lost so many times before. And when they lose yet again, it breaks their heart. After enduring this experience 100 times in a row, you'd think Cubs fans would learn their lesson. But that's what's so tragically amazing about these folks—they don't. They just keep hanging on to hope.

The following is your guide to feeling like you just bought the winning lottery ticket, even though you haven't and most likely never will. Because who knows? Maybe if more people lived like Cubs fans, the world would be a better place. Probably not, but there's a chance, right?

CHAPTER 1

There's Always Next Year (TANY)

Or next week. Or next whatever. That's the beauty of having the Cubs fan mentality. What happened last time around has no bearing on what could happen in the future. It's like waking up every day with a completely new start. No matter how horrible today was, tomorrow is sure to be better. Take love, for instance. Maybe you've never had a meaningful relationship in your entire life. Conventional wisdom says you probably won't have one next year, either. Screw conventional wisdom. Let's not forget that this is the kind of wisdom that said man couldn't go to the moon and dogs couldn't talk. One of those things has already occurred, which means it's just a matter of time before Butch can ask you about your day when you get home from work.

Unlike conventional wisdom, Cubs wisdom says anything is possible. Sure, the Chicago Cubs haven't won a World Series title since 1908. And yes, that's almost a century. But instead of focusing on the annual letdown, Cubs fans look to next season to find solace. If they ever actually dwelled on the drought between championships, they'd probably jump off the Tribune building with notes that have the words "I give up" scrawled on them attached to their shirts.[1]

Cubs fans have come to depend on TANY, and never was this more evident than in November 2003. The Cubs were just weeks removed from the most agonizing collapse in team history—which is saying something, considering this team's history—having blown a 3–1 National League Championship Series lead to the Florida Marlins. The turning point of the series came in the eighth inning of Game 6, when infamous Cubs fan Steve Bartman interfered with left fielder Moises Alou, causing him to drop a foul pop off the bat of Marlins second baseman Luis Castillo. Whether the ball was actually catchable will never be known (replays suggested it was), but one thing is clear: something happened when that baseball ricocheted off Bartman's outstretched hands. A shroud of silence rolled over Wrigley Field, and it seemed Cub Nation knew it was about to be left at the altar yet again.

Castillo ended up walking, and the dramatic shift in momentum sparked an eight-run Marlins rally from which the Cubs would never recover. The North Siders had entered the inning up 3–0, with their ace Mark Prior on the mound. By the time Castillo popped to second for the third and final out of the frame, the Cubs were down 8–3. After dropping Game 6, they were pounded 9–6 in Game 7. The Marlins went on to beat the New York Yankees in the World Series.

---

1. Given the pathetic 2006 Cubs season, it's possible that someone will have actually offed himself in this manner by the time this book is printed. Apologies in advance to any affected relatives.

The headphoned Bartman bungled his way into Cubs lore on that fateful night in October 2003.

The Cubs went home.

What should have followed was mass suicide. Under brand-new manager Dusty Baker, the Chicago Cubs had come within five outs of the promised land, only to have their hopes dashed once more. The fragile hearts of Cubs fans had been pushed to the brink and then ground to a pulp. Immediately following the 2003 season there was plenty of the inevitable commiserating and talk of the big "what if," but that kind of defeatist thinking was gone by November, when TANY hit Wrigleyville like a 1960s Christian revival.

Goin' Deep:
The Philosophy of Next Year

When it comes to TANY, Cubs fans have solid support in the annals of great thought. Scottish philosopher David Hume thought it erroneous to assume that since something has always happened the same way that it will continue to do so. Just because the sun has risen every day since the beginning of the earth, it doesn't necessarily follow that it will rise again tomorrow. There's simply no proof, no definitive way to be sure, that the sun will rise.

Now, let's apply this notion to the Chicago Cubs. It might sound naïve, but I challenge anyone—especially Tony La Russa or Ken Williams—to prove the Cubs will not win all 162 games next season. Sure, it seems easy. After all, the average Cubs roster is filled with guys who wouldn't even crack most Triple-A lineups. But because the future is not bound to the past, it's entirely impossible to prove the Cubs won't go undefeated Next Year. You can't even prove Roberto Novoa will continue to suck, despite an established history of consistent suckage.

Of course, it should be noted Hume did believe that to ignore all these sorts of connections would be downright silly. He would likely assert that while the Cubs' legacy of failure isn't causing their continued troubles, we should keep an open mind in "conjoining" these consecutive years of disappointment.

But in fact, it doesn't stop with Hume. Cubs fans can also take consolation in one of the central dictums of the philosophy of this very subject—that is, correlation does not imply causation. For instance, say that a bell in a Chicago factory rings every day at 5:00. Meanwhile in Milwaukee, workers at a different factory leave their jobs at the same time so they can get loaded on Pabst Blue Ribbon at the local Brewers bar and feel better about their lame city. The two events seem to be related, but did the bell in Chicago cause the workers in Milwaukee to begin drinking? Of course not. Similarly, with the dawn of another baseball season, astute observers might conclude that because the season is starting, it follows that the Cubs will fail to win the World Series. This is pure fallacy! As logical as it might seem, the mere fact that the Cubs are playing does not imply they will lose.

Intelligent people agree: There's Always Next Year.

Suddenly, Next Year was going to be the one all over again. Every Cubs fan was sure of it.[2] The 2003 team had collapsed in the playoffs because they were inexperienced. In 2004, with the same personnel, they would most certainly soar to their first pennant since 1945 and their first World Series victory since 1908. TANY didn't just make it

---

2. A little story to illustrate the far-reaching effects of TANY: I have an extremely disconnected "granola" friend in Los Angeles. Up until 2003 he knew nothing about baseball, let alone the Chicago Cubs. He had never even heard of Sammy Sosa. That changed during the 2003 NLCS, when the Cubs suddenly became a national phenomenon for their great play—and ultimate demise. After they lost to the Marlins, my friend said to me, "This means next year is the year, right?" Which is a pretty remarkable thing to hear from a guy who couldn't tell you how many runs a grand slam scores.

possible, TANY made it inevitable. The spread of TANY grew so much over the winter that even *Sports Illustrated* picked the Cubs to win the World Series in 2004. Next Year was finally here.

Well.

It wasn't, of course.

The club didn't even make the playoffs in 2004. But that only underscores the amazing power of TANY. Any person in his or her right mind should have known the Cubs would not be successful in 2004—that's what happened, after all—but TANY forced everyone to think differently, and it made for a more enjoyable season.

Likewise, just because you've been emotionally challenged every day of your life up until this morning, that doesn't mean things can't turn around. Tomorrow is a new day! And if you don't fall in love tomorrow, may I remind you of next week? Nobody knows what's going to happen a week from Tuesday, which means it's entirely possible love could happen. You could sit down on the bus next to the man or woman of your dreams. You just have to hope. What else are you going to hope for? Lonely nights? Sad holidays? Yeah, that's a great existence. Excuse

Cubbie Kid

you while you cry yourself to sleep on a huge pillow made of microwave dinner receipts.

In addition to nullifying past tragedies and providing for a hopeful tomorrow, TANY is a great excuse, so you should feel free to use it liberally in your everyday life. If you don't do a good job on your TPS Reports this year, just tell your boss they'll be accurate Next Year. When people ask why you live in a conversion van, simply remind them that life is a marathon, not a sprint. "There's Always Next

Practical Application

Problem: You didn't get the big promotion at work.

Solution: Don't worry about it. If you had received the promotion today, you wouldn't have anything to strive for tomorrow. Remember: the thrill is in the chase, whether it be for a World Series title or a slightly bigger cubicle. Achieving your goal will only force you to come up with a new goal, and that can be pretty daunting. Just look at the Boston Red Sox. After winning the championship in 2004, what's their goal now? To win it...again? Doesn't sound too exciting, does it?

Clearly, this all makes sense in the abstract, but you may be thinking it doesn't do you any good in real life. Hoping for the promotion Next Year won't get you more respect. It also won't give you the raise you need to afford a shiny new sports car. But neither will being sad about not getting the promotion this time around. Did you ever think about that, smart guy? So you can either get depressed about being passed over or you can look at the bright side and say, "Hey, maybe I'll realize all my dreams Next Year." At least you'll be in a good mood the next 12 months.

Year," you could say. "I guarantee my home won't have wheels in 2008."

TANY can also help prepare you for the worst before it happens. In 2004 Cubs fans were already using TANY when the team

Did You Know?

Independent studies have shown that Cubs fans can deal with disappointment better than any other social group in the United States.

was tied for the wild-card lead with just a week left in the season. The ballclub had been sliding precipitously, so instead of waiting for the Cubs to fall short of the playoffs, fans knew what to think: TANY. That way a playoff berth would have exceeded expectations, while a playoff miss (what actually happened) didn't hurt so bad. In short, TANY takes away the sting. But don't take a Cubs fan's word for it. Try it out yourself. This January, when you don't keep your New Year's resolution to drop 10 or 15 pounds, satiate yourself with a big éclair and a nice dose of TANY.

And it doesn't have to be TANY all the time. It could be TANJ, for when you lose your job to outsourcing. Or TANL, for when you need a liver transplant because you took chapter 2 of this book to heart.

Perhaps the most important aspect of this "next" philosophy is that it doesn't involve the "how" factor. If you tell a friend you're going to be a more attractive person Next Year, he or she may ask you exactly how you plan to achieve that. Who cares? The point is that you'll be more attractive, dammit. Cubs fans don't ask themselves how the team is going to assemble a World Series roster during the off-season. That would completely undermine TANY by creating doubts and concerns about the future. Besides, the "how" can be figured out later because Next Year is great for that, too.

Chapter 1

Quiz

1. You just found out your spouse wants a divorce. You should:
   A) Jump off a bridge
   B) Murder said spouse for insurance money
   C) Denounce all members of the opposite sex
   D) Hope for a more committed mate next time around

2. What's the best way to deal with mounting credit card debt?
   A) Declare bankruptcy
   B) Promise yourself that you'll pay off your bills Next Year
   C) Borrow money from a close friend or relative
   D) Rob a bank and/or convenience store

3. Which of these statements is accurate?
   A) Live for today
   B) Live for tomorrow
   C) Bobby Hill was underrated

Answers
1. D; 2. B; 3. B

If Not Soriano, Beer Will Make It Better!™

On November 19, 2006, the unthinkable happened: the Chicago Cubs spent some serious cash. Perhaps scared by the fan apathy produced by a 96-loss season, the Tribune Company splurged, authorizing Cubs GM Jim Hendry to give Alfonso Soriano an eye-popping $136 million contract. It was the fifth-largest contract in major league history. To many people around Chicago, acquiring one of the best hitters in baseball was a sign of better things to come: wins, division championships, maybe even a World Series.

But better things don't always happen in Wrigleyville, a place where even Soriano might end up hitting .240 with 12 home runs. Indeed, as every Cubs fan knows, there's only one surefire way to make things better: drinking beer.

This seems like an obvious one, but too many Americans ignore the magic of beer. Whether they've turned to prescription drugs like Prozac and Oxycontin or simply prefer to wallow through their misery as sober fools, they're underestimating just how good you feel when you're drunk. Even a slight buzz can turn the biggest frown upside down. Just ask former Cub Todd Hundley.[1]

A primary reason for the Cubs fan's fascination with beer is location. Chicago is a beer-drinking town, nestled in the heart of the Midwest. If ever there was a part of the country that could use a couple drinks to make things a little more interesting, it's a state like Illinois. Flat land can make you extremely thirsty. The same can be said for daily life in any of Chicago's suburbs, nice, boring places like Schaumburg and Naperville that have more shopping malls than residents per square mile. Of the 35 billion gallons of beer consumed annually in the world, roughly half of them are imbibed in the greater Chicago area, you gotta figure. In fact, it's not uncommon for some midwesterners to have a few Bud Lights before heading off to work, or if it is uncommon, it doesn't seem so. Chicago is a lot like Boston, if Boston could handle its liquor.

But why?

Why does Chicago love beer so much? Theories abound. One suggests it's much easier to handle the ridiculous Chicago climate under the influence of alcohol. If you're over the age of eight, you simply can't be sober and happy in 10-degree November weather. Luckily, beer has a way of warming up the extremities. Some people even believe that Chicago's fondness for alcohol can be traced back to the 1920s, right about the time the Cubs began finding themselves on the wrong side of a winning record with unfortunate regularity. This seems the most likely scenario.

---

1. If you think this is a cheap shot, you obviously never hung around Piano Man Lounge on Clark Street after Cubs home games in 2001 or 2002.

No matter the reason, the bottom line is that Chicagoans from 79th and Phillips to Sheffield and Armitage all enjoy downing a few pints every four or five hours. With the swilling gene already in them, Cubs fans have taken beer drinking to epic proportions. Part of it is recreational (nothing says baseball like a $5 Old Style, except maybe a $6 Budweiser), but the majority of the boozing is therapeutic in nature. Cubs fans have discovered one of life's irrefutable truths: Beer Will Make It Better!™

It doesn't even matter what *it* is. Who worries about a three-run deficit in the bottom of the ninth inning when they've had 12 beers? It's enough to keep your eyes open at that point.

Did You Know?

When you black out, you don't remember anything, including all of your problems.

Practical Application

Problem: You feel old.

Solution: Try a drinking game. Nothing makes you feel young and immature like a good round of Quarters. If you're drinking alone, maybe the Hour of Power is more up your alley. The point is that just because you happen to be old, it doesn't mean you have to feel that way. Every drunk person in the world acts the same age: 18. The more beers you drink, the closer you get to that age. If you're 21, it only takes one or two. But if you're 43, it'll be a good eight or nine bottles of Miller Lite before you're running naked through Wrigleyville, wishing you were back in college.

Goin' Deep:
Plato Was a Lush for a Reason

Legendary Greek philosopher Plato is credited with perhaps the most inspired drinking quote of all time: "He was a wise man who invented beer."

Unfortunately, Plato didn't elaborate on this belief in any of his writings, suggesting he may have uttered the famous phrase moments before getting annihilated at the local bath house with a few of his students. Still, Plato clearly ascribed to the Beer Will Make It Better!™ philosophy, as the following fictional-but-entirely-probable dialogue demonstrates:

Final Lesson

Plato: Well if it isn't Aristotle, my favorite pupil. This is quite the rager you've thrown for my retirement.

Aristotle: I just hope we have enough beer.

Plato: Simple Aristotle. In this day of strife, persecution and abhorrent hygiene, can you ever really have enough beer?

Aristotle: No, I suppose not.

Plato: Indeed. Consider that my final lesson. You are now ready to be a great philosopher.

See? Even way back in the 4th century BC, the world's finest minds knew the magical qualities of beer. One can only imagine how drunk Plato would get if he was a modern day Cubs fan.

Notable Quote

Question: What's wrong with Chicago Cubs fans?

Konrath: There is absolutely nothing wrong with Cubs fans, and Cubs fans have no problems with anyone else. Of course, this is only true after a 30-pack of Old Style.

—author J.A. Konrath

The following is what typically happens during a game at Wrigley Field. The opposing team scores more runs than the Chicago Cubs. This results in what baseball purists call "a loss." Losses can be depressing, especially if they are the kinds of losses the Cubs bring upon themselves. These involve mental errors, physical errors, blown saves, runners left in scoring position, strikeouts, missed signs, wild pitches, passed balls, double plays, injuries, managerial mistakes, poor relay throws, and awful base running. The cumulative effects of such blunders could ruin anyone's day. So why do Cubs fans always seem so happy after their team suffers yet another agonizing defeat? Booze.

There are approximately 1,924 pubs and taverns within a three-block radius of Wrigley Field, and each is stocked to the brim with ice-cold beer. From tallboys of domestic swill to Stella Artois on tap, Cubs fans have a myriad of options to lift their postgame spirits. It's pretty difficult to care about $\frac{1}{162}$ of a season when you're sucking down the sweet nectar of the gods alongside a throng of cheerful yuppies—many of whom are scantily clad women you just know would be willing to go home with anyone with a pulse.

While beer might not be the long-term answer to all of life's problems, it's the perfect short-term solution to quite a few of them. This is not strictly a modern phenomenon. The ancient Egyptians, the first beer drinkers in recorded history, knew the benefits of a good brew. After all, nothing helps you unwind from a long day slaving at the pyramid like a nice, lukewarm jug of Tutankhamen's Best.[2] The Egyptians also drank beer to make themselves feel better about not having cable television and proper  plumbing. In medieval times, the French were known to get sauced on a regular basis, probably to make up for a lack of women who shaved their armpits. Many people in France drink for similar reasons today. Likewise, beer can help you deal with your own daily annoyances. Maybe you aren't happy with your job, your car, or your spouse. Not to worry. Beer will make them all better! Beer can turn your sad, rusty Chevy into a...well, you won't be able to see the rust, anyway. And when was the last time you

---

2. Unless you preferred Sphinx Light, of course.

heard a drunk guy complain that his lady wasn't hot enough for him? Never. Just like beer makes a blown save acceptable, it makes an ugly girlfriend or wife acceptable, too. The opposite also holds true: any average, balding Joe can be as smooth as George Clooney if you look at him after 60 ounces of Heineken.

Top 5 Beers Cubs Fan Love

5) Bud Light—You can't get more American than the King of Beers, but you also can't drink 12 regular Budweisers in seven innings (it's way too filling), so Cubs fans often choose the Light version, which will get you just as drunk with half the calories.

4) Heineken—Cubs fans know the best way to impress the ladies is with a high-class foreign blend: a Mai Tai. The second-best option is an import beer, and this is the only one they sell at Wrigley—unless you count Guinness, which they probably give away free in the skyboxes to "friends of the Cubs" from companies like Boeing and Accenture.

3) Pabst Blue Ribbon—Sure, it might be the most bitter beer this side of Keystone Light, but at least there's a fancy blue ribbon on the can. That screams quality.

2) Old Style—It's local. It's bad. It even comes with instant "saloon breath." What more could 40,000 drunk fans ask for?

1) "The Special"—All other beers pale in comparison to whatever costs the least—or comes cheapest by the bucket.

"But how can beer actually make my life better?" is what you're probably thinking.

Technically, it can't. It simply creates the illusion of betterness. And illusion is the foundation of every Cubs fan's approach to life.

So drink up! That's what they do in the bleachers.

Chapter 2

Quiz

1. You just got fired from your job as a bank teller. What's the first thing you do?
   A) Purchase a shotgun at the nearest Wal-Mart
   B) Tell your spouse
   C) Update your résumé
   D) Get so drunk you can't remember why there's a cardboard box with all your work stuff on the bar stool next to you

2. How many beers does it take for a 200-pound man to forget all his problems?
   A) 11
   B) 8
   C) 2
   D) 5

3. Which of these statements is accurate?
   A) Beer just makes things worse
   B) Not having beer just makes things worse
   C) Being sober is fun!

Answers

1. D; 2. A; 3. B

The Heckler

Everybody Needs a Scapegoat (Or Even Just a Goat)

When the Chicago Cubs didn't make the 2004 playoffs because of a 2–7 record over the final nine games of the season, it wasn't the fault of Sammy Sosa, Kerry Wood, or even LaTroy Hawkins, the team's combustible closer. Nor was it because easygoing manager Dusty Baker failed to press the right buttons down the stretch.

According to Cubs fans, it was all because of a billy goat named Murphy. If you believe the legend, this smelly, lovable farm animal has been behind every Cubs collapse over the past six decades, causing blown saves, botched ground balls, and various other forms of North Side choking.

And did I mention that this goat's been dead for more than 50 years?[1]

For all you non-Cubs fans who happen to be gleaning this book for valuable life lessons, here's the abbreviated story of what happened the last time the Chicago Cubs played in the World Series, from Wikipedia.com:

---

1. Presumably.

William "Billy Goat" Sianis, a Greek immigrant who owned a nearby tavern, had two $7.20 box seat tickets to Game 4 of the 1945 World Series between the Chicago Cubs and the Detroit Tigers and decided to bring his pet goat, Murphy, with him. Sianis and the goat were allowed into Wrigley Field and even paraded about on the playing field before the game before ushers intervened. They were led off the field. After a heated argument, both Sianis and the goat were permitted to stay in the stadium, occupying the box seat for which he had tickets. However, before the game was over, Sianis and the goat were ejected from the stadium at the command

The late Bill Sianis's nephew, Sam (left), and his son, Tom, bring a descendent of Bill Sianis's infamous goat to Wrigley Field prior to the start of a game on October 14, 2003. Don't believe in karma? The game played that night is now known as the Bartman Game.

Practical Application

Problem: You accidentally ran over the neighbor's cat.

Solution: Wow, that's a tricky one. On the one hand, your neighbor deserves the truth. On the other, it's not like anyone's going to launch a full investigation to see who did the poor kitty in. Here's what you do. First, you utilize a scapegoat to make yourself feel better. In this case, the obvious cause of the problem was the cat, who never should have been mingling around your driveway. Unfortunately, while blaming the cat will improve your mood, it probably wouldn't do much for your neighbor's disposition, so now you'll need a secondary scapegoat. Not to worry. The answer is written all over the cat: tire tracks. Those tires could belong to any of the cars that have driven up and down the street today. So just put on a sympathetic face, knock on your neighbor's door, and calmly explain that you saw a large SUV hit their cat in the middle of the street (where you just finished moving the cat with a shovel). This way your neighbor knows his cat is dead, but the two of you can still be friends.

of Cubs owner Philip Knight Wrigley due to the animal's objectionable odor. Sianis was outraged at the ejection and placed a curse upon the Cubs that they would never win another pennant or play in a World Series at Wrigley Field again (Sianis died in 1970). The Cubs lost Game 4 and eventually the 1945 World Series; worse yet, following a third-place finish in the National League in 1946, the Cubs would finish in the league's second division for the next 20 consecutive years, this streak finally ending

A black cat was to blame for the Cubs' 1969 late-season collapse, so when Jeromy Burnitz spotted this feline at Wrigley Field in June 2005, the Cubs threw in the towel en route to a 79–83 season.

Notable Quote

Question: Do you believe in the Curse of the Billy Goat?

Mantegna: I don't believe there's a curse. There's an aura of defeat over the team. It's been there for nearly 100 years. It's tough. It makes a huge mental block. In terms of the Cubs, as close as they come, they get a crack in the dike, the trickle of water becomes a flood. You sit there and ask, "Can this be?" But it can be overcome. It's got to be. We wouldn't be Cubs fans if we didn't believe.

—celebrity Cubs fan Joe Mantegna

in 1967, the year after Leo Durocher became the club's manager. Since that time, the cursed Cubs have not won a National League pennant or played in a World Series at Wrigley Field—the longest league championship drought in Major League Baseball history.

As interesting as that may be, most people don't really believe some Goat Curse is keeping the Chicago Cubs out of the fall classic. But we're not dealing with most people, are we? We're dealing with Cubs fans, the same folks who blame their team's 1969 collapse on a black cat and the 2003 downfall on an overzealous fan in the stands. Should you ask them to clarify either of those debacles, the die-hard Cubs faithful would probably claim the goat was somehow behind both, haunting the franchise from the big petting zoo in the sky.

The point? It doesn't matter if the curse is plausible. All that matters is that Cubs fans are more than willing to believe in it, giving them the power to blame anything on

Top Five Cubs Curses You Didn't Know Existed

5) The Curse of Tommy John—Every year at least one Cubs pitcher must undergo (or be returning from) this very serious elbow surgery. Recent victims include Kerry Wood, Jon Lieber, Scott Williamson, Ryan Dempster, Rod Beck, Will Ohman, and Chad Fox. The curse has even affected nonpitchers, like frequent Cub Tony Womack.

4) The Ghost of Gary Scott—The most famous Cubs bust who's not named Corey Patterson, Gary Scott, is still alive, but his spirit has found a way to kill the future of every position player prospect who has dared to don Cubbie blue since the early 1990s.

3) Cell Phone Arm—One of the few curses that afflicts the fans, Cell Phone Arm forces seemingly normal people to flail like wild monkeys when they're told (by the person they're on the phone with) that the WGN cameras have found them.

2) The Cash-Cow Curse—As long as the Cubs continue to be a limitless piggy bank for team ownership, with the fans filling Wrigley Field rain or shine, nothing will change. Except maybe the amount of advertising sold in the ballpark.

1) Wrigley Field Goggles—Beer goggles have nothing on their baseball-based cousins, Wrigley Field Goggles, which make 40,000 people watching bad baseball think they're watching good baseball just because they happen to be sitting in a historic ballpark.

a scapegoat. Which, in this case, just happens to be an actual goat.

You, too, can employ this tactic in your life. From your own shortcomings and mistakes to random acts of God, you'll soon be able to gloss over the real causes of your problems. The first step is to come up

Did You Know?

In the late 1980s, a popular Milli Vanilli song prompted many people to blame all their problems on the rain. It didn't work, and one of the guys in the duo ended up killing himself because of it. Lesson? Never blame it on the rain, just to be safe.

with a scapegoat. It can be a person, an inanimate object, or perhaps a memory from your childhood.[2] In a perfect world, the scapegoat would somehow relate to the problem, but it's not always necessary. If baseball outcomes can be blamed on a dead billy goat, surely your troubles can be blamed on...your overbearing boss.

You got in a car accident on the expressway? Well, maybe if you weren't so angry at your stupid supervisor at work you would have been able to focus on the road and avoid the crash.

Your wife overcooked the chicken? Of course she did. How was she supposed to know your boss would keep you at work so late? Call it the Curse of the Boss, and blame him for your sudden weight gain, too. It might not fix the

---

2. Memories from your childhood should be saved for extreme circumstances, like when you're accused of murder. Because if you try to claim that your dad forcing you to hunt when you were 12 somehow caused you to run that red light back there...it probably won't work. But it'll make a lot more sense if you're accused of being a sniper.

problem, but it sure will make you feel better about eating yet another chocolate cupcake for breakfast.

If it sounds silly or trite or just plain dumb, you're missing the point. Blame first. Ask questions later. Let's say you just got dumped. Would you rather face the fact that you and your aforementioned face are totally undesirable or blame the whole thing on the mirror you broke in the bathroom that morning?

Chapter 3
Quiz

1. You passed gas in the elevator. What do you do?
    A) Claim responsibility for that bad boy
    B) Start whistlin' "Dixie"
    C) Hit the emergency stop button
    D) Ask the guy next to you if he had burritos for lunch

2. If you get caught cheating on your spouse, you should:
    A) Blame it on evolutionary instincts
    B) Call it the Curse of the Broken Zipper, then shrug
    C) Denounce the devil for making you do it
    D) Any of the above—they're all great

3. Which of these statements is accurate?
    A) You have nobody to blame but yourself
    B) Everyone's a suspect but you
    C) Honesty is always the best policy

Answers
1. D; 2. D; 3. B

The **Heckler**

It's Not Over until You're Mathematically Eliminated

How long can you hold out hope?

If you're like a Cubs fan, as long as the numbers allow. For the past five decades, these people have been waiting until the last possible moment before declaring it time to get ready for Next Year. The Cubs could be 19 games behind the St. Louis Cardinals with just 20 games to go, but they've still technically got a shot to make the post-season. It's still mathematically possible, and that's what truly matters.

When I was a kid, I was a master of holding out hope. While all the White Sox fans in the family[1] were busy making fun of me for still believing in my beloved Cubs at the end of August (any August, unfortunately), I was diligently working the math.

---

1. Sadly, I come from a broken baseball home. My mom's side of the family is all Cubs, and my dad's side is all Sox. I was actually a White Sox fan until 1983, when I abruptly switched allegiances and decided to start rooting for the Cubs. This was due in large part to the fact that I was only six and had no rationale for doing anything. Much of the blame also belongs to WGN.

Cubs fan Michael Toth of Wilmette, Illinois, works on a formula on August 5, 2006, that would lend support to the Cubs playing baseball in October. Unfortunately, his theory was soundly refuted by mid-September.

"If the Cubs win 20 in a row and the Cardinals lose 19 of 20, we would be in first place," I'd say. "Providing the Cincinnati Reds play at or below .500 for the next three weeks."

It might seem a little far-fetched to an outsider, but Cubs fans know the twisted logic only too well. Had I shared such calculations with other "believers," they probably would've given my formulas serious consideration. And why not? It all made sense on the page. By removing variables like players and injuries and poor coaching, all that was left were the numbers. Numbers that could be worked, massaged, and twisted to help my team reach the postseason.

Before you question my methods, consider my madness: if there's one thing Cubs fans understand, it's knowing exactly when their team has officially been eliminated from the playoffs. Years of evolution have made this an innate ability. As I write this very sentence, the Cubs are 13 games behind the Cardinals and 21 games under .500, and it isn't even the All-Star break. To some, the 2006 season is over. To the math, it's Central Division all the way, baby! There's still half a season left, which is plenty of time for the Cubs to make up 20 or 30 games, let alone a measly baker's dozen.

So how does this help you? How can the fuzzy math of being a Chicago Cubs fan change your life? Easy. It will give you hope. But not just a little bit of hope. You probably have that much already, even if you're a Milwaukee Brewers fan. I'm talking about a boatload of the stuff, enough to combat a lifetime's worth of insurmountable odds. Imagine a more confident you, a you that laughs in the face of failure right up until the moment you actually fail. The lesson here isn't to devise mathematical equations that will make it possible for you to land that perfect job. That really wouldn't work. The moral of the Cubs fan's story is to believe as long as possible, which in itself is a noble goal.

Practical Application

Problem: You're a 35-year-old female, and you're beginning to think you'll never get married.

Solution: Actually, you're pretty much mathematically eliminated at this point. Refer to chapter 2.

Goin' Deep: You Can't Mathematically Eliminate Logic

L et's take a detour into the world of logical possibility. Again, Cubs fans can breathe easier thanks to the work of thousands of philosophers who have dedicated their lives to thinking through these issues. This is a simple synopsis, but, in logic, philosophers break down propositions like this:

True propositions: These are true in the actual world, the world we know (i.e., "The Cubs did not make the playoffs in 2006.").

False propositions: These are false in the actual world, the world we know (i.e., "The Cubs won the World Series in 2006.").

Necessary propositions: These are true in any world that we can imagine (i.e., "All unmarried men are bachelors.").

Impossible propositions: These cannot be true in any world we can imagine (i.e., "Ryan Theriot and Ronny Cedeno are both taller than each other at the same time.").

Now take the proposition, "The Cubs and the Brewers must each win the 16 games they play against each other if the Cubs are to make the playoffs." Ridiculous. In any world we can imagine, it cannot be possible that the Cubs and the Brewers each win the games they play against each other—it's illogical.

It's an impossible proposition.

> However, let's look at the proposition, "The Cubs will win the next 29 games, which will allow them to make the playoffs." Granted, this may be a false proposition—I mean it seems unlikely, after all—but it's not an impossible proposition. We can imagine a world in which it could be that this proposition is the case. So, you know...you never know.
>
> This world might also be one in which Jacque Jones actually hits an 0–2 pitch.

Let's say you're an unemployed investment banker, seven days removed from an interview with Goldman Sachs, and you still haven't heard back—even after you sent a brilliantly worded thank-you email. Two things are happening here. One: you really want the job. It's Goldman Sachs, the New York Yankees of the financial investment industry. And two: you are starting to worry. By any measure, a full week is a long time not to hear anything regarding your status. Prospective employers don't usually make their favorite candidates wait, so the odds of you sitting in a corner office in Manhattan anytime soon are pretty remote.

Screw the odds.

What have they done for you lately? Probably less than Janet Jackson, and clearly not enough if you're still unemployed. But instead of giving up on Goldman Sachs, hold out some hope. Maybe all the top decision-makers are at another one of those corporate get-togethers in the Cayman Islands. Or maybe there's a bitter power struggle going on as the executives decide who to hire, with three people in your favor and just two holdouts left. While

Bleacher Bum

there's only one possible negative reason you haven't been contacted by your interviewer (you aren't going to be hired), there are literally thousands of possible positive reasons to hold out hope. In order to make room

Did You Know?

Unbeknownst to Cubs fans, Magic Number refers to the number of games you have to win to decide whether you'll be playing in October.

for your fabulous new salary, they could be dispensing with a few superfluous vice presidents and their huge bonuses. They could be preparing your office; marble floors take time to install. It's not entirely inconceivable that they have already hired you—you just don't know it yet. At least that's what you should be thinking, because your goal is to postpone giving up as long as you can.

That way, when your friends and family ask how the job search is going, you can honestly tell them you're awaiting good news from a certain company called Goldman Sachs. Maybe they've heard of it? Yeah, that's right. You bet they have. And what happens if another prospective employer calls two weeks from now? Normally, you wouldn't mention the fact you didn't get the last job you interviewed for. But if you think like a Chicago Cubs fan, you could say something like this:

"Oh, hello KPMG! I'd love to interview with you. I expect to hear back from Goldman Sachs about a recent meeting that went extremely well, but I've always been interested in talking with you guys. The timing couldn't be better."

You see? It's that easy.

Chapter 4

Quiz

1. It's been two whole days, and the jury is still out. You should:
   A) Decide whose "girlfriend" you want to be in prison
   B) Change your plea to, "Just sentence me already!"
   C) See if that involuntary manslaughter offer is still on the table
   D) Assume they're debating between not guilty and "way innocent"

2. Why hasn't your date from last week called you back yet?
   A) You smell funny
   B) Nobody wants a crazy person with a glandular problem
   C) You have all the personality of a rock
   D) He/she has been out of town on business and is bound to call any minute now

3. Which of these statements is accurate?
   A) It's not over until the fat lady sings
   B) Who cares about a fat lady?

Answers

1. D; 2. D; 3. B

Winning Really Isn't Everything

From overzealous NBA fans to angry Little League parents, America is officially obsessed with winning. These days, being a good sport isn't nearly as important as throwing batteries onto the field or knocking out the teeth of the guy whose kid just struck out your son to end the game.

While the rest of the sports world descends into a mess of riots, shouting matches, and obscene gestures, one group of folks is just happy to be at the game: Cubs fans. Oh, sure, there are a few bad apples in every bunch. But just because a couple hundred angry bleacher fans who aren't willing to put up with the constant losing decide to boo and throw empty beer cups onto the field, that doesn't mean it's representative of all the fans at Wrigley. They don't call it the Friendly Confines for nothing.[1] Most Cubs fans are way more accepting of failure, so they just sit there enjoying baseball, good or bad. And for the first time in recent history, the downtrodden are the only ones who have it right, because they're the only ones who are still

---

1. Actually, as you'll learn in the "Cubs Fan's Glossary" at the end of this book, "Friendly Confines" is probably a nickname given to Wrigley Field by opposing teams because it's so easy to win there.

having a good time, win or lose. Cubs fans understand there's more to baseball than winning.

Like eating an entire tray of cheese-drenched nachos in one inning. Or finding out the paunchy fan next to you has been to 184 home games in a row and has missed only nine contests in the last decade. That's interesting stuff, and it can make an otherwise sorry loss worthwhile. You might even get to hear firsthand about a game the Cubs actually won. Too many people think the final score determines the overall experience of the game, as if the Chicago Cubs losing 8–2 somehow turns a sunny day gray or negates the great time you had drinking Old Style with your friends all afternoon long.

Winning really isn't the only thing. It's a bonus.

Some people might argue that a fan who roots for a losing franchise isn't a very smart fan, but you have to be

So what if the Cubs are losing again? You can't get nachos like these at home. *Photo courtesy of Getty Images.*

pretty crafty in the head to continually enjoy Cubs baseball. The team goes out of its way to make the people in the stands miserable, and the fans keep finding ways to enter and

Did You Know?

Losing doesn't make you a loser unless you were a loser to begin with.

leave the Wrigley Field gates with smiles on their faces. Who do you think is smarter? The New York Yankees fan, who can't be happy just getting to the World Series, or the average Chicago Cubs fan, who can somehow manage to have the best summer of his life watching his team finish 17 games out of first place?

Which brings us to the statement you probably expected to see much earlier in this book: life is like baseball.[2] Just as people lose sight of what's truly important when it comes to sports, so, too, do they miss the point in everything else. What it means to "win" in life is different for everybody. For a person living in rural Ohio, it might mean keeping the farm in the family for one more generation. For a 21-year-old Northwestern graduate living in Wicker Park, it could be landing a job with IBM, Citibank, or some other stuffy company that pays exceedingly well. My friend is a good example, actually. For the purposes of this book, let's call him Jake. Jake wants to be a rock star. He's played the guitar since he was 11 years old in the hopes of someday jamming on a stage in front of 50,000

---

2. If you were waiting for something hilariously negative about White Sox fans, you can find that in chapter 7.

Goin' Deep:
Is Struggling a Good Thing?

Even in the worst sorts of hell, shreds of solace can sometimes be found. Consider French existentialist author Albert Camus's take on the myth of Sisyphus. Sisyphus, a terrible murderer, was condemned to an eternity of pushing a giant boulder up a mountain only to have it roll back down each time he reached the top. Camus was using the analogy to describe modern life (he was discouraging suicide), but if this sort of fate doesn't adequately fit the futility of Cubs fandom, I'm not sure what does. I mean, you have a doomed soul, an eternal struggle, and a baseball-shaped object. The only thing missing is a few injured pitchers by the names of Mark and Kerry.

Anyway, despite Sisyphus's existential horror, in the end Camus argues that it's the process itself—the rolling the rock

up the hill—that gives meaning to his life. So while the end result is meaningless (the rock is going to roll back down just as surely as the Cubs will crumble), the eternal struggle is the very point of it all. Which

French existentialist writer Albert Camus gestures as if to say, "What's done is done, there's always next year." *Photo courtesy of Bettmann/CORBIS.*

may explain why so many Cubs fans show up to games in September even when the club is 12 games out of the wild-card spot.

One cautionary note, however: Camus did think this angst-ridden existence was best kept to the back of our minds. While our day-to-day struggles may be the only point to life, it's probably not wise to contemplate them.

people. Then, after the show, he would love nothing more than to go backstage and have sex with eight or nine groupies.

Jake currently works part-time as a UPS package handler. In between night shifts down at the distribution center, Jake plays shows at local venues like the Elbo Room, Beat Kitchen, and the Cubby Bear. Now, Jake could let this get him down. To him, winning is playing the big stage with the postshow sexfest, and to the best of my knowledge, he's yet to sleep with groupie number one. By any stretch of the imagination, Jake is losing, or at least tied. If Jake were living life like a Yankees fan, he probably wouldn't be too happy. In fact, he might have ended it all years ago. Yet that's hardly the case. The last time I saw Jake, he was rip-roaring drunk and smiling from ear to ear. Why? Had he finally booked that gig at the United Center? Had the White Stripes personally requested that he open for them? Nope. He was just happy about the three-day weekend. It was a holiday, you see, and Jake likes to sleep in. It sounds trivial, but that's the whole point. While Jake could be busy hating his "losing" existence, he's having a ball. Jake's

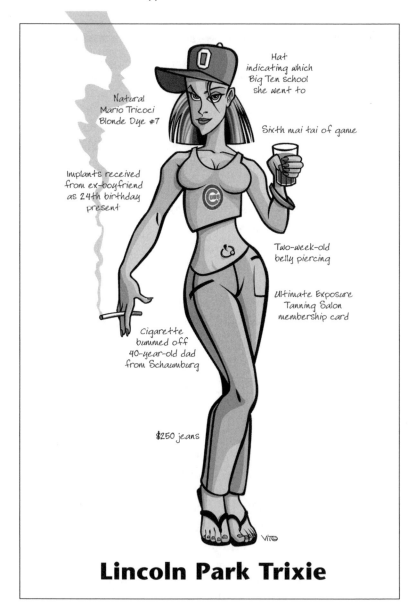

Lincoln Park Trixie

extra four hours of holiday sleep are the Cubs fan's tray of nachos.

To paraphrase a famous quote: it isn't whether you win or lose, it's how much you enjoy the game. If you're not careful, you could get so wrapped up in losing that you don't even appreciate the game itself. And by game, I really mean life, if you haven't figured that out already.

Chapter 5

1. That guy in the SUV beat you to the parking space. This means:
   A) You should give up now and drive home like the failure you are
   B) He's the only one getting groceries today
   C) Life has frowned on you
   D) You get to spend more time in your air-conditioned car

2. Which of these statements is accurate?
   A) If you don't win, you lose
   B) If you don't win, you're still drunk and/or have a belly full of cotton candy

Answers

1. D; 2. B

Loyaltiness Is Next to Godliness

Nobody likes a traitor. Whether you're an international spy who turns on your native country or a Chicago Cubs fan who decides to start cheering for the St. Louis Cardinals, there is absolutely no honor in switching sides. Sure, it would be nice to root for a team that actually wins more often than it loses, but changing allegiances is a serious offense that will ultimately leave you feeling hollow and dirty.

At the very least, it will alienate you from your friends. One day you're wearing Cubbie blue, and the next day you've got an Albert Pujols jersey on your back. What are your friends supposed to take away from that, other than the fact you clearly have no character and are completely untrustworthy. And for what? A cheap thrill? One of the biggest misconceptions in life is that the grass is always greener on the

The newlywed Burtons of Vincennes, Indiana, show that—although rare— mixed marriages can work.

other side. But sometimes it isn't. Sometimes it's covered with weeds and dog shit. Coincidentally, that kind of grass can often be found in Missouri. Now, obviously, there are clear benefits to being a Cardinals fan. The winning. The professional play. The joy of heckling lesser teams.[1]

But it's not all great. Much like Chicago White Sox fans, the people of St. Louis have their own stigmas. They

---

1. Admittedly, this is one benefit that would almost be worth switching allegiances for—but only almost. In 2006, for example, the Cubs were the worst team in the National League. This meant North Side fans couldn't even heckle the Brewers or Pirates, and that's just sad.

Sad but True (but Really Fake) Loyalty Factoid

Unfortunately, according to an online survey done by theheckler.com, Chicago was home to 1,174 defections in 2005 following the White Sox's impressive march to and through the World Series. While the majority of Cub Nation remained steadfast in its loyalty to the one true Chicago franchise, some fringe fans were taken in by the surprising South Siders. The amazing offense, timely pitching, and couldn't-miss coaching were exactly what these North Side fans had been looking for in a team all their lives. Manager Ozzie Guillen's charisma alone was responsible for nearly 500 of the conversions. Conservative estimates suggest 80 percent of those defectors will regret their decision within five years, but by then it will be too late, as they will already be covered in tattoos.

The unfamiliar glitter of a world championship was too alluring for more than 1,000 defecting Cubs fans in 2005.

Did You Know?

Treason is punishable by death in all 50 states, including Illinois. And Chicago is in *Illinois*.

are seen (mostly correctly) as overweight yokels, and the only positive thing these overweight yokels have in their lives is the Cardinals franchise. Is it really worth a few more victories a season to be associated with these people? This Cubs fan doesn't think so.

Regardless, say you do make the change. After a particularly excruciating home losing streak against the New York Mets and Arizona Diamondbacks, you decide enough is enough already, and you buy a Cardinals hat. Congratulations, you're now an overweight yokel.

It gets worse, though, because breaking loyalty in one area of your life shows people what you're really made of: wishy-washiness.

Imagine the parents of your godchild trying to trust you with the care of their newborn baby, while at the same time wondering if you won't just find a better godchild instead, one that's cuter or doesn't smell so much like feet. Or imagine your spouse wondering if you'll trade him or her in the first chance you get. Or imagine your boss not giving you the big promotion because he just doesn't feel like he can trust you anymore.

And for what? A cheap thrill?

If you live like a Cubs fan, however, you don't run the risk of alienating anyone, because you will embody loyalty in all its forms. So the next time you pledge your devotion to a loved one, you must honor that pledge, no

Earrings that have been in family since last Cubs World Series

Maximum strength bifocals

Blissfully smiling through 8-run loss

Lightweight jacket worn in "chilly" 90-degree weather

15 pieces of Cubbie flair

Neatest scorecard in stadium

One wrinkle for each year Cubs haven't gone to playoffs

Wrigley Granny

matter how many times he disappoints you. You also won't turn your back on an alcoholic friend. Hell, you won't even turn your back on a friend who stole your lawnmower. That's how dedicated you should be. Remember, loyalty isn't always pretty, but it certainly beats the alternative: wishy-washiness.

Chapter 6
Quiz

1. You're thinking of becoming a St. Louis Cardinals fan. You should:
   A) Totally go for it, and buy some overalls while you're at it
   B) Reconsider, because being a Cincinnati fan is pretty sweet, too
   C) Buy a kitchen knife with a Cardinals logo on the handle, then stab all your friends in the back with it
   D) Have a few more beers. There's Always Next Year

2. Which of these statements is accurate?
   A) Friends don't let friends switch teams
   B) Friends are for suckers!
   C) Friends are not nearly as important as Albert Pujols

Answers

1. D.; 2. A

The
Heckler

At Least You're Not a Sox Fan[1]

No matter how bad it gets for Cubs fans, it could always be worse. They could be White Sox fans. True, the White Sox won the World Series in 2005, ending an 88-year drought between championships and stomping all over the hearts of Cubs fans in the process. It was an exciting season for the South Siders as their team was in first place every day of the year, then went on to march through the playoffs with a 15–1 record. The pitching was sensational, with the Sox starters going deep into every ballgame and actually completing four games in the NLCS against the Anaheim Angels. This was especially difficult for the Cubs faithful to swallow; we were supposed to be the ones with the pitching. Unfortunately, the North Side is home to more pitching busts than Coors Field. So on the one hand we have the Sox, World Champs. On the other end of the spectrum we have the Cubs, who most certainly did not win the World Series in 2005. Or 2006. Or any other year since 1908. This should make it infinitely better to be a White Sox fan right now.

---

1. Zing!

Sox fan William Ligue had himself something of a Bartman moment when he inexplicably ran onto the field and attacked Royals first-base coach Tom Gamboa in 2002.

Not to be outdone, this Sox fan tried to bag a Royals first-base coach of his own the following season.

Only it doesn't.

There are three reasons for this. First, rooting for the Sox is not without its disadvantages. The moment you put on a White Sox

Did You Know?

The average Sox fan spends at least six months of his life in prison.

jersey, you must also put on the stigma that goes along with it. When you walk down the street, people in Chicago no longer think of you as a normal person. They think of you as a stereotype: poor, obnoxious, blue collar, uneducated, and ready to rush the field so you can attack a Kansas City Royals base coach.[2] You are a threat to society, capable of wreaking havoc at a moment's notice. Now, to be fair, not all Sox fans fit that profile. I once heard about a Sox fan who almost finished community college.[3]

See?

See that joke I made?

South Siders get no respect in this town, especially from North Siders like me. My own father is a White Sox fan, yet I have no qualms lumping him in with the rest of them (so long as he doesn't read this book—sorry Pops!).

The second reason it's no fun being a Sox fan is simple: only like five or six of them have been around

---

2. For more info, simply Google "William Ligue."
3. This Sox fan was named Joey Malonecki. Sadly, he was just two semesters short of graduating when he impregnated his girlfriend, Desiree, forcing him to quit school and get a full-time job at a local hardware store. On the bright side, he didn't have to worry about studying during the 2005 playoffs. He spent all his time gettin' ripped!

since before October 2005. While Wrigley Field routinely sells out, U.S. Cellular Field is one of those places where you can hear your voice echo, like in an empty hallway or a bathroom. Despite the fact that they were in first place the entire 2005 season, the White Sox rarely sold out the stadium, probably because so many people were worried about being associated with everyone else at the park. "Oh, I'm not that kind of fan," the casual White Sox fan often tells himself. "I'm different."

Unfortunately, they're the only ones who think that.

The last (and most important) reason it's tough being a Sox fan is that it means you can't be a Cubs fan. In Chicago, you are one or the other. Period. And while we've already discussed what a Sox jersey suggests about the person wearing it, a Cubs jersey suggests just the opposite: Cubs fans are seen as wealthy, well-mannered, white collar, and educated. And it's all true!

See?

Practical Application

Problem: Someone just stole your car.

Solution: The fact you even had a car in the first place means you're way better off than those people who ride bikes all over town and then claim they're doing it by choice. "I could totally afford a car if I wanted," one of those bikers might say. "I just prefer being sweaty when I arrive at work, home, or anywhere, really." So at least you're not a pathetic biker. Besides, you have insurance, right? So what's the problem?

There I go again.

But forget Sox fans. Let them write their own book if they care so much.

The point is that no matter how many losses the Chicago Cubs rack up, no matter how many games their bullpen blows, no matter how many times they send fans home wondering what could have been, no matter the final score, no matter the weather, no matter the history, no matter the fact it's July and their season is already over—no matter any of that and so much more, I can always take solace in my Cubbie blue. Because unlike the Sox fan, I have plenty of brethren. Millions of them across the nation. If I move to a new city, you can be sure there's a Cubs bar in town. Unless that new city

Notable Quote

Question: Was there ever any doubt between being a Cubs or Sox fan?

Garlin: When I was a kid, I went to a game at Wrigley, and they wouldn't let me bring in my bottle of water. I got so angry that I burned my Die-Hard Cubs Fan Card, and I swore off the Cubs for the Sox. That didn't even last a month.

—*Curb Your Enthusiasm* star Jeff Garlin

is Cicero or Beverly, Illinois, the same can't be said for White Sox fans.

Another good thing: nobody asks me if I drive a Chevy Camaro when I put on my Cubs jersey.

They don't expect me to appreciate their mullets, either.

Being a Cubs fan in Chicago is a little bit like being a handsome older brother. You get all the attention, while the mongrel eight-year-old gets all the dirty looks.

The lesson to be learned from this is simple. There's always someone out there who has it worse than you.

So you think you're a few pounds overweight? Just imagine what it must be like to be one of those people who has to purchase two seats on the airplane because they can't control their Kentucky Fried Chicken intake. At least you're not that guy. At least you're not the guy on the plane with halitosis, either.

Nine out of 10 psychiatrists do not endorse the "Sox fan comparison" as an official treatment for depression, but they should. If 10 shrinks ever actually heard about it, this Cubs fan has no doubt they'd get all their patients on

Top Five Most Common Sox Fan Baby Names

5) Hope
4) Randy
3) Staci
2) King
1) Destiny

board immediately. The following are just a few times when this technique can lift your spirits.

If you think you're ugly, just be glad you're not Lyle Lovett.

Got no money? Hey, at least you have a house that isn't made of cardboard, like that guy in the alley next to Starbucks.

Just got fired? Yeah, well you could be Julie from accounting, who had to sleep with Dan "Back Moles" Borden to keep *her* job.

No matter how bad the situation gets, at least you're not a Sox fan.

Chapter 7

Quiz

1. You just got voted "Least Likely to Succeed" by your high
    school class. You should:
    A) Try to make the best of it by being the biggest damn
        failure ever
    B) Satiate yourself with a dozen codeine tablets
    C) Prove them wrong by applying to Harvard, despite your
        1.74 GPA
    D) Be glad you weren't voted "Least Likely to Marry," like that
        loser Theodore Rosenblatz

2. You're the only one in the office who didn't get a raise. This
    means:
    A) You suck at your job
    B) You should really stop getting in at noon
    C) Your stupid boss has it in for you
    D) You should still be happy, because at least you aren't a
        nine-year-old Chinese kid blow-torching the soles onto
        Nikes for 50¢ an hour
    E) All of the above

3. Which of these statements is accurate?
    A) At least White Sox fans get to watch a winning team
    B) White Sox fans are too busy changing my oil to have time
        to watch the game

Answers

1. D; 2. E; 3. B

The Power of Low Expectations

A wise man once said: "When you hope for the best, anything less sucks."[1] That man was right, because the easiest way to make sure you aren't happy with a particular challenge in life, whether it be a baseball game or an SAT exam, is to place too much faith in a positive outcome.

Chicago Cubs fans know this, which is why they expect to lose every single game. Their team could be up four runs going into the ninth, but the seasoned fan knows a loss is still pretty damn likely, so he doesn't get his hopes up. It's called the Power of Low Expectations.

"Wait, wait, wait," you say. "That's not called the Power of Low Expectations. It's called 'the Cubs are awful.'"

Sure, if you're talking about any year since 1945, the Chicago Cubs may indeed be awful. But if you think that's why their fans have low expectations, you're missing the point. Any team can be bad enough to inspire a defeatist attitude, yet it is a uniquely Cubs phenomenon to trample a fan's hopes and dreams. Consider the Pittsburgh Pirates,

---

1. It's possible this has never really been said by anyone.

One of the hallmarks of being a Cubs fan is keeping the proverbial bar low. If you don't expect every routine ground ball or fly ball to be handled, you won't be so disappointed when one gets away.

Practical Application

Problem: The sex wasn't that great.

Solution: What did you expect? You think just because you're cheating on your spouse it's going to be a wild, passionate romp? Those kinds of things only happen in movies, not in room 12B of the Motel 6 on Roosevelt Road. Perhaps you should simply try to be happy about the fact that you still have the ability to pull off an affair without the help of Cialis.

a positively woeful franchise ever since the departure of superstar slugger Barry Bonds. The team has made no effort whatsoever to improve, giving its small fan base no reason to expect a winning record. It's safe to say the constant losing has created a defeatist attitude in Pitts-town. Pirates fans have been conditioned to expect at least 90 losses per season and thus are content to wallow in mediocrity. When the Pirates get swept three series in a row, the fans don't flinch. Nobody ever promised them a playoff run. There have been no Mark Priors, Kerry Woods, or Corey Pattersons in the Pirates farm system. And the last time they were a factor in the postseason, it was because they traded Aramis Ramirez, Kenny Lofton, and Randall Simon to the Cubs, who came within five outs of the World Series (but didn't make it, of course).

There's something much different going on in Wrigleyville, and luckily, Cubs fans have learned to combat it. This problem is commonly referred to as optimism, and it's caused by everyone from Cubs GM Jim

Question: If there were a big book of something based on the Cubs, what would it be?

Neyer: *Big Book of Dashed Hopes.* There's no reason why this team hasn't won more pennants over the years. The fan base is there.

—ESPN writer and *Big Book of Baseball Blunders* author Rob Neyer

Hendry to the oddsmakers in Las Vegas casinos. Every year, it seems, the Cubs purport to have a chance at winning a championship. All they needed was a consistent third baseman—and now they have him! Meet Gary Scott,[2] circa 1992. The Cubs finished that season in fourth place, 18 games out of first. All the Cubs needed was some playoff experience—and now they have it! Say hello to your 2004 Chicago Cubs, who finished in third place, 16 games out of first, despite just missing the World Series in 2003.

But it was no biggie, at least not for Cubs fans.

We stopped believing the hype decades ago and have learned the Power of Low Expectations. It goes like this: never expect to win. Consider a simple example.

Pretend it's mid-June, and the Cubs are two games in front of St. Louis in the NL Central. (I know this is hard, but really pretend your ass off.) On this particularly pleasant summer evening, the Cubs are playing host to the

---

2. Hailed by baseball experts as a can't-miss prospect that would finally restore order to third base for the Chicago Cubs, Gary Scott played just 67 games in parts of 1991 and 1992. He notched a .160 batting average in 175 at-bats and was quickly demoted to the minors. He would never make it back to the big leagues.

Top Five Reasons to Be a Pessimist

5) By always viewing the glass as half-empty, you always have a reason to get another beer.

4) Sure, good things come to those who wait—in ketchup commercials!

3) If you expect to fail, then the act of failing could really be viewed as...success.

2) Optimism is so '90s.

1) Hope gets shot down all the time, but when was the last time you heard of someone's apathy being trampled?

Pittsburgh Pirates, the aforementioned punching bag of the National League. The grand old scoreboard in center tells us the Cardinals have already lost their game, meaning the Cubs can separate themselves from the Redbirds if they can just hang on to the three-run lead over the Bucs. Considering that—in this hypothetical situation—the Cubs have won their last eight games, one is tempted to expect a victory. Did I mention we're in the eighth inning already, and a healthy Mark Prior has only surrendered two hits thus far?

You couldn't possibly imagine a better scenario for the Cubs, and that's exactly your problem. Instead of looking at the negatives, you've been caught up in the emotions of the moment and have allowed your expectations to be raised. You expect the Chicago Cubs to win. Over the last

Did You Know?

John Kerry actually expected to win the 2004 presidential campaign. Ouch.

90 years, how many times have the Cubs put distance between themselves and whoever was in second place? What are the odds, given his history, that Mark Prior will stay healthy? What are the chances of the Cubs winning nine games in a row? And finally, now that you're so sure of a victory, how much more will it hurt when they lose?

If only you had reined in your expectations. It's infinitely easier to watch the Cubs blow a game in the late innings when you kinda thought it was going to happen anyway than it is when you thought they were going to win. Both losses hurt, to be sure, but at least one doesn't leave you absolutely crushed.

The same can be said for your career.

After years of being taken for granted by your manager, the old bastard finally retired. With him out of the picture, you were so sure your new boss was going to make everything better. Yep, you'd finally have a chance to shine under this new guy, who gave a totally convincing and motivating speech to the department his first day in charge. But that's not how it worked out, is it? Instead, you got your hopes up for nothing, as the new boss turned out to be even worse than the old boss. Now look at you, more disgruntled than ever and you still have to photocopy tax receipts for a living.

Another great example of the dangers of unrealistic expectations is marriage.

We've finally reached the point in this country where over half of all marriages end in divorce. Let's all pause a moment, as Americans, and congratulate ourselves for yet another achievement in the field of pursuing our own happiness. The key words here are *our own,* as in not yours. It's gotten so bad you can't even depend on parents to suffer through a rotten marriage for the sake of their children anymore. What's this world coming to?

With a divorce rate topping 50 percent, maybe it's time everyone just lowered their expectations a little bit and agreed to stay together until "something" do us part. You're really setting yourself up for failure if you mention the whole death thing. Surviving better, richer, and good

Being a Cubs fan is like getting married. If you go into it expecting a bitter divorce from the start, anything else feels that much more special.

health is a breeze, but if you think you'll make it through worse, poorer, and sickness just as easily, you need to lower the bar because it's not going to happen. Another thing that won't happen is you being able to cope with your divorce if you never thought it was going to occur in the first place.

Confused?

High expectations can do that to a person, leaving you dizzy with feelings of disappointment, failure, and angst. In the future, just expect nothing. You won't be disappointed.

Chapter 8

Quiz

1. The asking price for your Wrigleyville condo is $280,000. This is:
   A) Exactly as much as you paid, and therefore appropriate
   B) Only half of what you could get if you played your cards right
   C) Ridiculous—they could buy three condos for that in Cicero
   D) Going to be really disappointing when you only get $220,000

2. Which of these statements is accurate?
   A) Expect the world
   B) Be happy with stale beer and a kinda-okay spouse

Answers
1. C, D; 2. B

CHAPTER 9

To Boo or Not to Boo

There comes a time in every Cub fan's life when his faith is tested. It's certainly understandable, given the many losing streaks he must endure just to get through each season. Hell, for some fans, this test comes after the very first time they root for the Cubs.[1] But somehow, the die-hard fan is able to rise above the 90 losses and come back Next Year, reenergized and ready for more.

It's a little something Cubs fans call "loyalty." You don't see much loyalty in sports today, with fans eager to jump ship at the first sign of a losing campaign. Take the New York Yankees, for instance. The team goes to the World Series just about every other year, but you wouldn't know it from the way the fans boo them when they lose two measly games in a row. And God forbid they lose three straight—that's cause for a mutiny. Now, some people will argue that Yankees fans just hold their team to

---

1. This happened to my friend Tom, who moved to Chicago from Texas and decided to become a Cubs fan. Unfortunately, the Cubs were blown out 10–1 in the first game he ever attended. They had three errors, one rain delay, and Sammy Sosa struck out four times. And while none of this is actually true, I'm sure you can imagine the scenario, which is what's truly sad.

a higher standard and the boos are their way of making it clear they've had enough of the mediocre play.

Those people are idiots.

Any fan who boos his own team isn't a real fan.

The majority of North Siders understand this. Sure, the last few seasons have brought a rash of boos from the home-field crowd, but they came mainly from the casual attendees, not the die-hards. An unfortunate side effect of a shrine like Wrigley Field is that it draws just as many people looking for a good time as it does people actually interested in watching the game.

The deeper issue is one of consistency. There's no honor in being a fair-weather fan. For those of you not familiar with the term, it refers to someone who is the biggest Chicago Cubs fan in the world when the team is playing well, yet will have nothing to do with the Cubs when they play like, well, the Cubs.

Notable **Quote**

Question: Being relatively new to the Cubs world, do you ever wonder how Cubs fans have managed to stick with it all these years?

Kasper: The thing you learn right off the bat is that although Cubs fans may not always be thrilled with what they see on the field, and they may think, "Here we go again," when something bad happens, they always care. And they care 365 days a year. Every other pro team in Chicago could win a championship in the same year, and the radio airwaves would still be filled with, "I'm concerned about the Cubs' fifth starter." If you're asking me to explain it, I can't, but I do think it's incredibly heartening that in today's disposable society, where everything seems to come and go very quickly, that a fan's bond to a team can remain so strong through a little thick and a lot of thin.

—Cubs TV broadcaster Len Kasper

Fans in the right-field bleachers litter Wrigley Field with beer cups and assorted other debris during an aggravating loss to the lowly Colorado Rockies in 1999.

Fair-weather fanning is an ugly thing to watch. Seemingly loyal fans suddenly go sour over a little 11-run outburst by the other team (as was the case on July 16, 2006, when the New York Mets scored 11 runs in the sixth inning, causing Wrigley Field to erupt in boos), or a routine five-game losing streak at the hands of lowly clubs like the Tampa Bay Devil Rays and Colorado Rockies. Next thing you know, foreign objects are raining down from the bleachers, along with a steady stream of boos and obscenities. Do these people have any idea how ridiculous they look booing the very player whose jersey they're wearing?

"You suck, Murton!" a fair-weather fan might yell at Cubs right fielder Matt Murton. "I can't believe I paid $75 for your jersey, you bum!"

Yeah, that'll show him.

But the main pitfall of being a fair-weather fan is simple: all of your previous suffering goes to waste. Any credibility

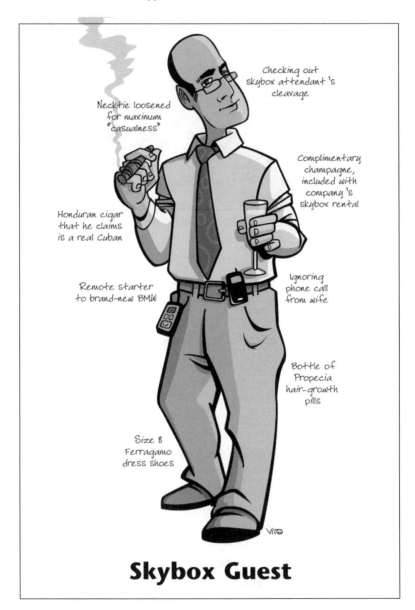

Checking out skybox attendant's cleavage

Necktie loosened for maximum "casualness"

Complimentary champagne, included with company's skybox rental

Honduran cigar that he claims is a real Cuban

Remote starter to brand-new BMW

Ignoring phone call from wife

Bottle of Propecia hair-growth pills

Size 8 Ferragamo dress shoes

Skybox Guest

you earned by agonizing through awful seasons like 1981 and 1995 is immediately erased from the record once you denounce the team in 2007. You become more than a joke—you become a traitor who can

Did You Know?

Some Cubs fans didn't even know how to boo their own players until relief pitcher LaTroy Hawkins joined the team in 2004. Those people learned fast.

never recapture the purity of being a true die-hard Cubs fan. This might not seem like a big deal, but it will be if the Cubs ever make it to the World Series. That's the single best thing about being a Cubs fan. There's no bandwagon. A team that hasn't won a title in nearly a century just can't have one. As a loyal fan of the Cubs, you can always claim you were there from the start. If by some stroke of luck the Cubs should happen to win it all during your lifetime, that phenomenon will end. The fan base will split in two: one half comprising true Cubs fans, the other a ragtag bunch of bandwagoners and opportunists.

Indeed, nothing in the history of civilization will have been more vindicating for any group of oppressed people than a victory in the World Series would be for Chicago Cubs fans.[2] Even Boston Red Sox faithful would have nothing on us. We would rule the sports world, and all other fans would envy our courage, our struggle, and most of all, our dedication. Who wouldn't want to be a part of that? You'd have to be dumb, or a White Sox fan, not to want in on that sweet action.

---

2. This may be an exaggeration.

Top Five Most Booed Cubs in Team History

5) Todd Hundley, 2001–02
   Reason: paid $6.5 million per year to hit like two homers
4) Malachi Kittridge, 1890–97
   Reason: couldn't hit his way out of a potato sack
3) Joe Carter (broadcaster), 2001–02
   Reason: he no talk very good
2) Steve Trachsel, 1993–99
   Reason: disappointing career, even by Wrigleyville standards
1) LaTroy Hawkins, 2004–05
   Reason: single-handedly ruined the 2004 Cubs season

LaTroy Hawkins had a particularly ignitable effect on fans at Wrigley Field.

Finally, how does this apply to life?

Oh.

It doesn't. I just wanted to get some things off my chest, and now that you've already read this chapter, there's nothing you can do about it. Now you feel like a real Cubs fan: a sucker.

Chapter 9

Quiz

1. The fan next to you is booing Cubs skipper Lou Piniella. You should:
   A) Disregard this entire chapter, and join right on in
   B) Pretend you don't hear him
   C) Politely ask him to keep it down
   D) Tell security you saw him buy beer for those minors over there

2. Which of these statements is accurate?
   A) You should only root for the Cubs when they win
   B) You should only root for the Cubs and whoever is playing the White Sox or Cardinals

Answers
1. D; 2. B

What Does All This Mean?

You're disappointed. I know. You purchased this guide to learn how to live your life like a Cubs fan, and all you got was a bunch of observations, clichés, and non sequiturs. You even got insulted once or twice. Maybe next time you should read chapter 8 first and work your way backward. That will give you just the perspective you need to fully enjoy this book.

Still, there's something else that's bothering you. You're wondering how all these ideas can coexist together. "How can you hold out hope for next year, yet not care if the team wins or loses?" you ask. "Then what the hell are you hoping for?"

That's an excellent, valid question. Admittedly, there isn't much rhyme or reason to any of it, almost as if the people living by these principles are crazy. News flash: they are.

Question: What was it like playing for the Cubs?

Banks: It's a part of me, like my family. People who come out here are like my friends; people that play here are like my brothers. It's just a total picture of my whole life, being at Wrigley Field, and being around the players and the fans. In my life playing here, I just learned to forgive and forget and go on and enjoy each day and each person that I'm with.

—Mr. Cub, Ernie Banks

And that's exactly how I described them in the introduction of this book. They're Cubs fans, and they're willing to abide by whatever principles get them through the day. Today it could be TANY. Tomorrow might be "Beer Will Make It Better!™" The end result is the ability to cope with a difficult situation. That's the real lesson to be learned from these noble folks. In the face of adversity, they do whatever it takes to keep themselves happy. We should all be that single-minded in life.

So now that you're armed with this confusing set of rules to live by, what next? The practical applications in this book will only take you so far. A more comprehensive look at the Cubs fan is needed to fully understand what makes him tick. To achieve this, I considered a few different routes. One idea was to interview famous Cubs fans, but then I realized famous people add something unquantifiable to the mix. They aren't typical Cubs fans. No matter how much they love the Cubs, people like Bill Murray and Jim Belushi have more important things to worry about than baseball. Most Cubs fans don't. So I only used a few insightful quotes from a select group of celeb fans. Hopefully they will inspire you to greatness, or happiness, or whatever else you're searching for in life.[1]

I also considered including a bunch of lists, like this one:

Top 10 Ways to Cook Dinner Like a Cubs Fan

10) While wearing your Ron Coomer jersey, because you sure as hell can't wear it in public.

9) Whatever you cook, make sure it's something that will leave a bad taste in your mouth.

8) Drink four beers before the water even starts to boil.

7) Refer to your kitchen as the Fridgy Confines.

6) Remind yourself it could be worse: You could be cooking like a White Sox fan, on one of those hot plates in the back of a house on wheels.

5) Predict greatness from your pasta, even though it's never been great before.

4) Buy all your ingredients from an overpriced Whole Foods, the Wrigley Field Premium Tickets of the food world.

3) Start everything off just right, then burn it. Burn it all!

2) Add a dash of Old Style, because Beer Will Make It Better!™

1) Prepare the worst meal ever, then promise yourself you'll cook something way better Next Year.

---

1. Unless you're searching for Scientology. I want no part of that.

Now that you've nearly finished this comprehensive guide, you are equipped with the tools to go out and enjoy life despite the heavy burden of being a Cubs fan.

But then I thought it might be cheesy to do everything in list form, so I only used five or six of those. Another option was to include articles from *The Heckler*. Those are always good for a laugh, but I don't know how much life guidance can be gleaned from an article about Lance Berkman mistaking Craig Biggio for a huge Twinkie (and subsequently biting him) or White Sox fans celebrating their winning record with a good old-fashioned tire

This pair of smiling Cubs fans traveled all the way to New York's Shea Stadium in hopes of seeing the team's first win of the season after 14 straight losses to start the 1997 campaign. Their wish was granted, but not until after the Cubs dropped the first game of the doubleheader.

fire. Plus, it would be a blatant plug for my newspaper, and I refuse to do that, even if it is the best satirical sports publication in the country. I mean, yeah, we get tons of press and people all over the nation love us, as evidenced by the fact we have subscribers in more than 40 states, but that has about as much relevance as the super-affordable subscription rate of $12 per season you can get by visiting theheckler.com.

That's www.theheckler.com.

At the end of the day, however, it seemed the best way to do justice to this lifestyle was to allow you, the reader, to take the principles at face value. Being a Chicago Cubs fan is a vague endeavor, after all. If you can somehow find a way to apply even one of these rules to your life, you've made progress on the road to happiness.

And if you think this is some sort of disappointing cop-out, welcome to the Cubs fan's experience.

If you have any questions about my controversial theories, life in general, or you just want to share one of your own Cubs-related anecdotes with someone who might actually give a damn, feel free to email me at george@theheckler.com. No White Sox fans, please.

The
Heckler

15 Habits of Highly Happy Cubs Fans

Life is a series of habits and routines repeated over and over again. Some people's habits include smoking, drinking, and playing cards. Other people have a routine that revolves entirely around eating: breakfast, something, lunch, something, dinner, something—and so on.

While no two Chicago Cubs fans are exactly the same, a majority of them exhibit broadly similar habits. In many ways, this is borne out of their collective outlook on life, as described in the preceding chapters. In order to better understand how the brain of a Cubs fan operates, and to put yourself in a similar mindset, you need to program yourself with some of their habits. The more habits you pick up, the more you begin to experience life as a Cubs fan. And the more you do that, the closer you will be to unlocking the true happiness inside you.

The following list is certainly not exhaustive, but it does give you a glimpse into the soul of the Cubs fan. Or something profound like that.

Habit 1: High-five more often.

This is not a new concept. Since the dawn of time, mankind has celebrated accomplishment through the slapping of palms. When the first caveman invented shorts by hanging a bush around his midsection, his hunchbacked friends were there to give him a high-five (at that point in the evolutionary chain, it may have technically been a high-four, but that would be a total digression). While the specific manner in which the high-five is executed has changed over the years—it was even the low-five for a while—the premise remains the same. You get so excited about something you can't hold it in any longer, and you slap hands with the person closest to you.

If you happen to be celebrating a home run at Wrigley Field, you usually don't even know who the high-fivee is. But at that moment, during that ritual smack of flesh on flesh, you form a bond with your fellow man. This bond not only reinforces your humanity, it allows you to make a positive connection whenever you please, and that's the kind of experience Cubs fans seek out in life.

Habit 2: Laugh in the face of adversity.

Not in the figurative sense, either. Cubs fans literally laugh harder the worse things get for them. Why? Because when the Cubs blow a ninth-inning lead for the third time in a week, you just have to smile. Sometimes, if you're faced with an irrational situation, the only rational response is to act irrationally.

Doctors have long held the belief that laughter is "the best medicine." Did you hear that? "Best medicine." Not "good medicine" or "okay medicine" or even "medicine you should only use as a last resort." So why deny your body and mind a good, healthy guffaw when it needs it the most? You know it makes sense. On its face, it might seem inappropriate to laugh when your boss fires you, but that's really the best way to deal with the situation. Crying won't get you rehired. Laughing will make you feel much

better immediately, and considering the fact you're now unemployed, you'll need all the positivity you can get.

Habit 3: Buy someone a beer.

Nothing will endear you to your friends and coworkers more than a nice, frosty beverage. That's why Cubs fans are always buying beer for each other. Every time a fan over the age of 21 leaves the Wrigley Field seating area, he or she returns with two cups of beer. It doesn't matter if the intended destination of the trip was the bathroom or the hot dog stand, the beer station immediately becomes a stop on the way. It's a simple rule: come back with an extra beer, or don't come back at all.

Imagine if everything worked like that. It's Tuesday, let's pretend, and the end of the week is but a mirage, a mere blip on the radar. You're suffering through another snooze fest of a meeting led by your moronic boss, when one of your coworkers returns from the bathroom with two bottles of cold, refreshing Bud Light.

Nice!

Your coworker has just earned your eternal loyalty with 12 ounces of hops, barley, and water. And if you return the favor, you, too, will have a friend for life.

Habit 4: Leave work early.

Wrigley Field didn't get lights until 1988, meaning every home game played during the first 74 years of the stadium was played during the day. While Wrigley is no longer light-challenged, the schedule still leans heavily toward 1:20 starts, and Cubs players are constantly grousing about all the day games on the schedule.

"I don't have time to sleep off my hangover," they say. "How am I supposed to play well on such little rest?"

To the fans, however, the daytime starts are a godsend because they give Chicagoans yet another reason to leave work early. Of course, the Cubs aren't the reason anybody actually gives their boss. Common reasons include stomachaches, family obligations, phantom funerals, and the ever-popular dentist appointment. I recently used a doctor visit. But the excuse is irrelevant. The bottom line is that being a Cubs fan gives you that much more incentive to get out of the cube and into life. So what if the Cubs aren't that great? Which would you rather do: watch the Cubs lose from the sun-splashed left-field bleachers or stare at a computer screen all afternoon while Big Brother breathes down your neck?

Habit 5: Throw it back.

When an opposing team's player hits a home run into the Wrigley Field bleachers, it doesn't stay there long. Tradition dictates that the ball immediately be tossed back onto the field. If it is not regurgitated in a timely manner, the surrounding fans join together in a relentless chant of "throw it back, throw it back" until the person holding the baseball is peer-pressured into sacrificing it to the bleacher gods.

As you might expect, this is a purely symbolic gesture.

The official scorer doesn't wipe the run(s) off the board when he sees the ball fly back onto the field of play. Nor is the opposing team discouraged from hitting more home runs into the stands.

So why, then, do Cubs fans get so excited about this peculiar practice of throwing it back? It just feels good. You dare to hit a home run off our pitcher? Screw you, pal! We don't need your pathetic baseball! In fact, you can have it back.

Juvenile?

Maybe.

Effective?

Big time.

The secret to ultimate happiness is denial. And denial can come in many forms, from throwing back a baseball to looking in the mirror and seeing 260 pounds of "thinness."

Habit 6: Heckle your rivals.

You should never let people get away with anything, even if they're just doing their job. As experts in the field of psychological warfare, Cubs fans understand how to get

inside an opposing player's head. This expertise comes from years of getting inside their own heads and reprogramming themselves to believe the Cubs have a chance to win the pennant. When this power is projected outward and focused on someone like Barry Bonds, the resulting heckles are truly inspired:

"Hey, Barry, what's your hat size?"

"Barrrrrroiiiiiidddds! Barrrrrroiiiiiidddds!"

"What's that sticking out of your arm?"

"Hey, Barry! I didn't think 'the clear' was illegal, either."

"Even your teammates hate you!"

"Hey, Bonds! I'm wasted!"

At first blush, these heckles could be construed as goofy or frivolous, but I assure you I have seen the power of these putdowns in action. Barry Bonds himself has given me the cold stare of death. Rickey Henderson flipped off my friend. Adam Dunn was surprisingly annoyed by our pleas to "stick a fork in him." If millionaire athletes can be rattled by heckling, so too can your rivals.

People like your mother-in-law. Your teacher. Or even your neighbor, who thinks he's so cool with his new car and his fake-breasted second wife.

"Nice replacement!" you could yell. "I got my wife right the first time, loser!"

Heckling isn't just fun. It's also therapeutic. Telling your nerdy coworker he's more like a "codorker" will make you feel better about yourself.

Habit 7: Overcelebrate.

Life is fleeting. One minute you're enjoying a juicy steak at Gibsons Steakhouse, and the next thing you know you're dead. Unfortunately, there's nothing you can do about your mortality, but you can enjoy the hell out of the time you have here on earth.

Cubs fans do this by celebrating everything that even mildly resembles a positive outcome. They celebrate mediocrity, like a 4–4 home stand or a third-place season. Cubs fans will go so far as to praise a swinging third strike. Sure, the player failed in his attempt to make contact, but at least he made it to first. That's something we can all appreciate.

This propensity to overcelebrate really irks non-Cubs fans. For some reason, it upsets them to see us North Siders enjoying a season full of miscues, blown saves, and runners left in scoring position. Those non-Cubs fans will

not die happy. What they don't realize is that life is short, and being miserable is a gigantic waste of time. It's like calculus that way.

It's not too late for you to learn this lesson. Whenever you get upset about your dismal career, celebrate the fact you have a career at all. That way, if you die of a sudden heart attack, you can at least say you died as the happiest septic tank cleaner ever.

Habit 8: If you have to pee, pee.

Cubs fans know better than to hold it. In addition to the damage waiting too long to pee can do to your bladder, it's just not very comfortable. This is the reason Cubs fans leaving Wrigley Field have no problem urinating in nearby alleys—it's the healthy thing to do.

So what if the people living in the apartments surrounding the stadium can't stand this practice? They knew what they were getting into when they signed the lease.

Habit 9: Pay too much for stuff.

Bleacher tickets. Domestic beer. Ryan Dempster jerseys. It doesn't matter how overpriced the particular item for sale may be, there's always a Cubs fan willing to buy it. Even the peanuts sold on Waveland and Sheffield, famously touted as "cheaper on the outside," can run you $5. Wrigleyville is like a mini-Manhattan, where saving money is not an option.

But it's not all bad.

It can't be, after all, if so many Chicago Cubs fans are able to stay happy amid the price gouging. So how do they do it? It's a matter of perspective. When you buy a six-pack of Old Style at the supermarket, you pay about $4.99. And that's exactly what it tastes like: $4.99 beer. When you spend roughly the same amount of money on just one Old Style at Wrigley Field, it tastes more expensive. Simply put, you appreciate a $5 beer more than you appreciate an 80¢ beer. The same can be said for a Derrek Lee jersey. If you only paid $10 for it, you might be tempted to use it as a washrag around the house, but the extra $60 makes it that much more special. Bleacher tickets are the best example of the effect of overpricing. The higher price makes the ticket seem more exclusive. So even though you're in the only section of the stadium that doesn't feature assigned seats, seatbacks, or roving beer vendors, the $75 you paid the scalper makes it feel like the best section in the house.

Habit 10: Don't ask questions.

Life is hard enough when you don't question everything. Why am I here? Should I go back to college? What the hell is that lump under my arm?

Cubs fans try not to be too inquisitive, because the answers to most of life's questions are not "you're rich!" or "there's an easy solution to your problems!" Nobody ever asks himself how to spend his vast fortune, either. That would be too easy. People ponder hard things, like how to make $800 a month feed a family of four or whether they can get cancer from their cell phone.

Who needs all that information?

A bleacher bum doesn't ask how a team with no bullpen is going to win 90 games this season. Nor does he inquire about the state of Mark Prior's shoulder. Such questions undermine the blind euphoria Cubs fans have come to know and love.

Habit 11: Wait in line.

If there's one thing that doesn't bother Cubs fans—aside from losing—it's waiting in line. And why should it? The things they stand in line for are usually worth the wait. Each February, for instance, the Cubs dispense thousands of bracelets with random numbers on them. A lottery is drawn, and the person with the winning bracelet gets the first opportunity to buy tickets for the upcoming season. Last year, scores of Cubs fans curled around the stadium in frigid temperatures just for the chance to buy Cubs tickets. To non-Cubs fans, this probably appears to be a gigantic waste of time, but those of us on the inside know it builds

character and is the only chance we have at beating the scalpers.

So we're okay with it.

Other things Cubs fans wait in line for are beer, the pisser, and entrance to the ballpark. All worthy causes. The lesson? If you have to wait in line, it's probably for something good. Think roller coasters, movie premieres, and dance clubs.

"But what about the DMV?" you say. "Why should I enjoy waiting in line there?"

That's a good question, and I could tell you there's a great answer for it, but I will instead refer you back to Habit 10.

Habit 12: Spend time in the sun.

Seriously. You need a tan.

Habit 13: Live life to the fullest.

Hot dogs. Nachos. Pretzels. Cotton candy. French fries. Peanuts. These are all things you should eat every chance you get. Even the slimmest of Cubs fans realizes the importance of inhaling as much food as possible over the course of nine innings. It may not be totally healthy for you, but it sure

is fun. And the best part is that it's guilt-free.

"Oh, I wouldn't normally eat six hot dogs and a lemon ice," you could say. "I'm only doing it just this once. I'm at the Cubs game, after all."

But you don't even have to be at the Cubs game. If you treat every day as a chance to enjoy the best life has to offer, then eat as many hot dogs as you want. If you're worried about being fat, don't be. Next to Green Bay Packers fans, Cubs fans are some of the fattest people on earth, and you don't see them worrying about it.

Habit 14: Sing drunk.

Much like the Wrigley Field bleacher section is the biggest singles party in America, the seventh-inning stretch is the biggest karaoke song since Neil Diamond's "Sweet Caroline." Every game, 40,000 people (attempt to) sing "Take Me Out to the Ballgame" in unison. Roughly half of these people are fall-down drunk, so the ensuing performance provides a pretty good show.

More important than the theatrics is the bonding experience. You've never really lived until you've sung arm-in-arm with your sloppy friends in the bleachers at

Wrigley. Something about the stadium, the tradition, and the booze forms the perfect milieu of happiness.

Milieu.

Look it up.

If Harry Caray taught us anything, it's that we should all sing drunk more often. So the next night you're out at the bar, drape your arm over the shoulder of the person next to you and belt out a few verses of "American Pie," "Sweet Caroline," or "Welcome to the Jungle."

Habit 15: Go nuts!

Cubs fans are crazy. You'd have to be to keep rooting for a team with a tradition built entirely on losing. Through it all, however, the smiles never fade. It could be the last month of an absolutely dreadful season, and Joe Cub Fan will still find a reason to be glad he's at the game or watching it on TV.

Does this make Cubs fans insane?

Yes.

Is that a bad thing?

Hell, no.

It's better to be nuts and happy than sane and sad. Whatever it is in the makeup of a Cubs fan that allows him or her to rationalize losing—and turn it into something positive—it's certainly a quality to be admired.

We should all strive to be more irrational. In fact, you should make it a point to do something irrational on a daily basis. Today it could be asking out that woman at work, even though she's already married. Tomorrow you could buy three cars, just because you have good credit.

Whatever makes you happy, no matter how crazy it sounds—that's the Cubs fan's motto.

A Century of Losing: 100 Years, 100 Frustrations

When the Chicago Cubs beat the Detroit Tigers in the 1908 World Series, they were probably feeling pretty good about themselves. Not only had they won two championships in a row—the Cubs defeated the Tigers in 1907 as well—the franchise had compiled an amazing 322–136 record from 1906–08. That's an average of 107 wins per season.

Little did the North Siders know, the 1909 campaign would kick off the most infamous championship drought in American sports history: 98 years and counting. With the Boston Red Sox finally ending their own drought (86 years) in 2004 and the hated cross-town rival White Sox ending theirs (88 years) in 2005, the Cubs are now alone in their misery.

So how did it ever come to this? How did the proudest franchise in the National League become the laughing-stock of professional sports? It hasn't just been the losing, although that surely would have been enough. It's also been the way the Cubs have lost and everything else surrounding the team. Cubs fans themselves don't even understand the extent of the damage; they just kind of sense its presence with them every summer. Outsiders have no clue. Oh, sure, most sports fans have heard of Steve Bartman and the 1969 Cubs, but that's just the tip of the iceberg with this franchise.

In order to fully understand how to live like a Cubs fan, you must first understand what it's like to be a Cubs fan. You must see what these people have been through over the last century. This section will touch on the major disappointments over the years, from the 1969 collapse to the Lou Brock trade to the renaming of the famous outfield bleachers.

1. Cubs' Monumental Collapse (1969)

The Cubs' strong 1969 season was the culmination of a five-year roster build-up by manager Leo Durocher. The team started off well, good enough to have an NL-leading 71–41 record on August 7. Yet the center did not hold for the Cubs when the team got into a race with the white-hot New York Mets in late August and early September. Stars Ron Santo and Glenn Beckert slumped, and "Mr. Cub" Ernie Banks had an appalling .186 batting average and hit only one home run throughout September. Chicago went 8–17 that month. While it's easy for statisticians to point the finger of blame at the Cubs offense, and superstitious fans to attribute it to the infamous "black cat" incident at Shea Stadium during a Cubs-Mets game, perhaps the one most responsible for the meltdown was the architect of the team. Durocher could be a very difficult manager to work with, as he confused berating his players with motivating them. In the face of the Cubs' difficulties in late 1969, all he could do was scold those around him. The season would eventually become known as "the one that got away."

2. The Bartman Play (2003)

Just five more outs. Wrigley Field was on the verge of erupting in celebration as the Cubs, leading 3–0 against the Florida Marlins in Game 6 of the National League Championship Series, looked to reach their first World Series in 58 years. In the eighth inning, Luis Castillo popped up a foul to left, and Moises Alou ran over to make the catch as the ball sailed toward the wall. But as Alou leapt to snag it, front-row fan Steve Bartman snatched the ball out of the air above Alou's glove. Cubs fans pelted Bartman with garbage as stadium personnel escorted him out of the park. It's uncertain whether Alou could have actually caught the ball, and Chicago still coulda—and shoulda—stopped the Marlins from subsequently scoring eight unanswered runs. The Cubs also could have stopped the Marlins from reeling off three straight victories to advance to the World Series. Yet Bartman is reviled among most of Cub Nation, which blames him for the team's failure.

3. Cubs Trade Lou Brock (1964)

If the 1969 season epitomizes the Chicago Cubs' penchant for failure, trading Lou Brock demonstrates the club's inability to recognize talent. The year was 1964, and the Cubs were in the midst of another losing campaign (76–86).

On June 15, they decided to trade Brock, a promising young outfielder, to the Cardinals. The most notable player they got in return was right-handed pitcher Ernie Broglio. It's unclear whether the Cubs were just tired of waiting for Brock to blossom or if they thought he never would. Either way, the deal is considered one of the worst trades in baseball history. Brock's accomplishments as a Cardinal border on comical: two World Series titles (the first of which came in 1964, the year he was traded), six All-Star appearances, Babe Ruth Award, Roberto Clemente Award, Lou Gehrig Memorial Award, Hutch Award, league leader in stolen bases eight times, and holder of a .391 career postseason average. In his 19 seasons, Brock accrued 3,023 hits and 938 stolen bases. He was a first-ballot Hall of Famer. As for Ernie Broglio, he spent two and a half seasons with the Cubs, going 7–19 with a 6.00 ERA.

4. Sox Fans (Since the Dawn of Time)

Superman has Lex Luthor. The Smurfs have Gargamel. And Cubs fans have Sox fans. A teeming mass of tattooed, mulletted hooligans, Sox Nation is the bane of every North Sider's existence. Even before their team won the World Series in 2005, Sox fans delighted in celebrating every Cubs failure over the years. In 1969, they rioted in the streets, probably. After the Cubs blew the 2003 NLCS, the most deafening roar didn't come from South Florida— it came from the South Side. And every time the Sox beat one of their American League foes, the fans leaving U.S. Cellular Field inexplicably chant, "Cubs suck." In addition to the baseball-related issues Cubs fans have with their crosstown counterparts, there's also the matter of crime. When a car goes missing on the North Side, you can be sure a Sox fan is behind the wheel. When someone mugs a guy in a Cubs hat, it could be random, but the odds say it was some Sox fan unhappy with how much more money the Cubs fan makes at his cushy white-collar job. Now, with a recent championship under their belts, Sox fans won't rest until they've ruined the lives of every die-hard Cubs fan in Wrigleyville.

5. Cubs Lose to Padres in National League Championship Series (1984)

It was finally going to be the year...and this time for real. Buoyed by Rick Sutcliffe's 16–1 record and future Hall of Famer Ryne Sandberg's breakout season, the 1984 Cubs ripped off an impressive 96–65 record, claiming the NL East crown. After winning the first two games of a best-of-five against the San Diego Padres in the NLCS, the North Siders needed one measly win to make it to the fall classic for the first time since 1945. But thanks to the TV network's demand for night games, the Cubs, whose record earned them the right to home-field advantage, would instead be forced to play three consecutive games in San Diego. They ended up losing all three, including Game 5, due (in large part) to a routine ground ball that went through the legs of first baseman Leon Durham. The Cubs wouldn't have another winning season until 1989, when they again failed in the playoffs.

6. Tribune Company Buys the Cubs (1981)

When real estate tycoon Sam Zell bought the Tribune Company in April of 2007, he vowed to sell the Cubs franchise after the season. While this laudable move will mercifully end the Tribune's reign of terror on the North Side, it doesn't undo the decades of hardship created by the Cubs' miserly parent company. Some wounds never heal, like losing Greg Maddux to free agency or bearing the sight of those damn Under Armour logos on the outfield wall. But the Tribune wasn't all bad—they did want the ballclub to be as profitable as possible. Those coffers had to be filled somehow, and people like Andy MacPhail and John McDonough made it happen by passing on the responsibility to the fans in the form of higher ticket prices, convenience charges, illegally scalped tickets, concessions and merchandise. Oh, wait. Turns out they really were all bad.

7. Cubs Don't Re-Sign Greg Maddux (1992)

In 1984 the Cubs signed a promising pitching prospect named Greg Maddux, and the rest was Chicago baseball history. Until 1992, that is. He tallied 20 victories and won the Cy Young Award that season, but difficulties with the Tribune Company over contract negotiations led to a move to Atlanta the following year. Maddux won 195 games over the next 10 seasons for the Braves, who notched 10 straight division titles and a World Series victory over that time span. And how did the Cubs do over that same period, you ask? One wild-card berth and one NL Central title. Maddux returned to the Cubs in 2004, but he was already past his prime, so while the signing conjured nostalgia for the fans, it failed to produce a championship on the field, let alone a playoff appearance. In 2006, with the team once again hopelessly out of the playoff race, Mad Dog was traded to the Los Angeles Dodgers, where he returned to young Maddux form despite his extreme old age.

8. White Sox Win World Series (2005)

Seeing one cursed team—the Boston Red Sox—victorious in the World Series before the Cubs was uncomfortable enough for North Siders. Seeing their crosstown rivals win it all the very next season was excruciating. Like the Red Sox, the White Sox had a curse rooted heavily in baseball lore. The "Black Sox" scandal of 1919 involved a payoff of key Chicago players, who threw the World Series against the Cincinnati Reds. As a result of the scandal, eight members of the Sox roster, including star outfielder "Shoeless" Joe Jackson, were banned for life. And so the legend began and was seemingly borne out by the team's drought of series victories between 1920 and 2004. However, they made the playoffs in 2005 with a tremendously talented roster and had home-field advantage throughout. To make matters worse for Cubs fans, the White Sox did absurdly well, executing one of history's most dominant postseason runs. They lost only one game before popping the champagne and hoisting the Commissioner's Trophy.

9. Cubs Lose to Detroit Tigers in World Series (1945)

It started innocently enough. The Chicago Cubs had just won 98 games—out of just 154. In the World Series, they faced off against their longtime rivals, the Detroit Tigers. Despite going only 88–65, the Tigers proved a formidable opponent, and the Series was extended to seven games. Still, the Cubs were favored to win. They had a vastly superior team and were not yet the punching bags of the National League. All that would change after Game 7, however, when they were blown out 9–3. The loss marks the last time the Chicago Cubs have been to the World Series. It also marks the start of the cursed era, thanks to the famous billy goat incident. Couple that with the beginning of the pennant drought, and 1945 is the defining season in Cubs history.

10. Ernie Banks Retires without Championship (1971)

More specifically, Ernie Banks retires without ever reaching the postseason. The Hall of Famer played 19 seasons, and not once did he get the chance to hit a home run in the playoffs or celebrate a National League pennant. It was the Cubs curse taken to the extreme: Even a player of Banks's caliber couldn't turn around a franchise that had long since lost its luster. Affectionately dubbed "Mr. Cub" by fans and teammates alike, Banks spent his entire career on the North Side. Unlike Billy Williams, Fergie Jenkins, and Ron Santo, Banks would wear no other uniform, for he was a Cub through and through. Which is why despite

512 home runs, 11 All-Star appearances, two MVPs, the Lou Gehrig Memorial Award, and a Gold Glove he has no World Series rings to show for it.

11. Ron Santo Not Elected to Hall (Multiple Years)

The biggest misconceptions about the outrage surrounding Ron Santo not being in the Hall of Fame are that it's purely Chicago-based or born entirely out of pity. Neither is true. While you could argue Santo deserves special consideration for battling type 1 diabetes throughout his career—doctors told him he wasn't going to live past 25 years old—he doesn't need the advantage. When he retired in 1974, he was arguably the second-best third baseman in history, behind Eddie Matthews. He went to nine All-Star Games and hit 342 home runs during an era known primarily for pitching (as opposed to, say, steroids). But it is defense that sets him apart from other third basemen. He won five Gold Gloves, led the league in chances nine times, assists seven times, and in double plays six times. So why isn't Santo in the Hall? He's a Cub. And the voters treat him like one, crushing his hope every ballot. Perhaps the most beloved of all Cubs players, Santo epitomizes what it means to be an eternal optimist in the face of eternal adversity.

12. Derrek Lee Breaks Wrist (2006)

All of the Cubs' hopes and dreams for the 2006 season rested on the bat and glove of All-Star first baseman Derrek Lee. Lee was not only the reigning NL batting champion, he was just the kind of player Cubs fans could rally around: humble, supremely talented, and durable. In his first seven years in the league, Lee had never been on the disabled list, and the Cubs were positive this trend would continue. That confidence was reflected in a five-year, $65 million contract the team gave Lee at the beginning of the season. But after a promising 9–5 start, Lee went down with a fractured wrist on April 20 in a game against the Los Angeles Dodgers. Rafael Furcal, who was barreling toward first base after a bunt, bulldozed him. The Cubs dropped 40 of the next 59 games they played while Lee watched from the dugout with a cast on his arm. Lee returned at the end of June. He played well, but went back on DL in late July. By the time he returned again in September, the team's fate had long since been decided.

13. Kerry Wood Undergoes Tommy John Surgery (1999)

More than three decades ago, pitcher Tommy John had a relatively new medical procedure called ulnar collateral ligament (UCL) reconstruction performed on his elbow. John gave his name to this kind of surgery, which would go on to become commonplace among major league pitchers who blow out their elbows. Enter Kerry Wood. Coming off a stellar Rookie of the Year performance in 1998, a season that saw the young phenom strike out 20 batters in a single game and lead the Cubs to the NL wild-card, North Side ace Kerry Wood was forced to undergo Tommy John surgery in the off-season. He missed all of

1999. Upon his return, the speed of his pitches was maintained, and he eventually made an All-Star run in 2003, but he was never the same, physically. The resulting string of injuries would turn Wood from a hero to a goat over the span of just a few seasons.

14. Cubs Lose World Series to White Sox (1906)

The inclusion of the Cubs' World Series loss to their crosstown rivals as one of the team's worst moments hardly needs further explanation. And yet, few people today understand how big a disappointment it really was. Perhaps it's the amount of time that's passed since it happened or maybe it's simply selective memory, but not many Cubs fans know this was a huge upset. Unlike today, the North Siders actually were the better team in the city in 1906—they led the league in team hitting, fielding, and pitching—and were therefore heavily favored to win against the White Sox. However, the Sox, dubbed "hitless wonders" because of their anemic offense, managed to hold their own against the Cubs. The two teams won alternately two apiece in the first four games of the Series, which surprised many fans for its competitiveness. But the Sox's "hitless" offense exploded at the end when they scored eight runs in each of their final two victories to win the Series, 4–2. Fortunately for the Cubs, they'd win the World Series two years later against the Detroit Tigers. Unfortunately, it would be the team's last title until, well, you know.

15. Gary Scott Is a Third Base Bust (1991–92)

When Ron Santo left the ballclub in 1973 (he retired in 1974 after one season with the Chicago White Sox), Cubs fans knew they were losing one of the best third basemen in the history of the game. What they didn't know was that the hot corner would turn into a virtual black hole for the next three decades, sucking up and spitting out Santo wannabes by the dozen. From 1974 to 2003, the North Siders went through 98 subpar players in an effort to find a serviceable replacement for the supremely talented Santo. From Steve Ontiveros to Manny Trillo to a guy nicknamed "the Penguin," the Cubs simply couldn't find a third bagger worthy of holding Santo's jock, let alone occupying his position. Then came Gary Scott. Hailed by baseball experts as a can't-miss prospect—Santo himself said Scott could ultimately restore order at third base for the Cubs—the young infielder played just 67 games in parts of 1991 and 1992. He notched a .160 batting average in 175 at-bats and was quickly demoted to the minors. Scott would never again set food on a big-league baseball field.

16. Line Drive Hits Mark Prior on Elbow (2005)

If the curse on the Chicago Cubs is real, then it's probably doubly true for the team's pitching staff. Take Mark Prior, for instance, a guy with worse luck than Ben Stiller's character in *There's Something about Mary*. In 2005 Prior began the season on the DL, as he would the following year. He did well when he eventually came back, though, building up a respectable 4–1 record in just a few weeks. Unfortunately for Prior, he started in a fateful game against the Colorado Rockies on May 27. In the fourth inning, Colorado outfielder Brad Hawpe sent one of Prior's pitches back to him in the form of a 117 mile-per-hour line drive that nailed him in the elbow—on his pitching arm, of course. The resulting fracture put him right back where he started the year, and he hasn't been the same player since. Well, unless you're talking about him getting injured every other day, he's the same player entirely.

17. Curse of the Billy Goat (1945)

Most Cubs followers have a passing familiarity with the curse that has afflicted their team for the past 60-plus years, and if they don't, shame on them. For all the Cubs fans who spend most of their time on cell phones or throwing up on someone else's shoes, here's how it went down.

William Sianis, who went by the nickname "Billy Goat," brought a real, live goat with him before the start of Game 4 of the 1945 World Series, in which the Cubs led the Detroit Tigers 2–1. Funny thing was, after Sianis paraded his goat on the field, the ushers escorted him off and didn't want to let him use the seats for which he had paid. Sianis and his goat eventually were allowed to use the box seats only to have Cubs owner Phillip K. Wrigley kick them out later in the game. When Sianis asked why, Wrigley replied, "Because the goat stinks." An incensed Sianis then gave up, but before he left, he declared that the Cubs wouldn't win another World Series until the goat was allowed in. Sure enough, Chicago lost that game and the World Series. After that year, they didn't make it back to the big one again, falling spectacularly short on a few occasions. Sianis even managed to get a zinger in a few weeks after the incident. Following the Cubs' collapse in the 1945 World Series, he sent a letter to Wrigley that asked, "Who stinks now?"

18. Cubs Sell Out with Ads Inside Park (2005)

An argument could be made that anywhere the words "Wrigley Field" appear within Wrigley Field, it's a kind of advertisement. After all, it's not only the name of the former owner, but also his chewing gum company. In fact, Wrigley Field was the first ballpark in baseball to take its name from a corporation. That claim aside, the park managed to stay remarkably ad-free over the years, especially around the diamond itself. As former Cubs president Andy MacPhail once said in an interview with *Sports Illustrated*, "I'm not really interested in putting up some jumbo sign in right field to get an extra $2 million to devote to the payroll. I don't think we have to do that to win, and I think if you do that, you lessen the uniqueness of Wrigley Field." Two years later the Cubs introduced Sears signage into the ballpark, and it's been a steady stream of advertising ever since: McDonald's, Culver's butterburgers, MasterCard, and United Airlines, just to name a few. The kicker came in 2005, when the Tribune Company added a rotating advertising billboard behind home plate, so everyone in the country would be aware that the team sold out. Thanks to the ads, Cub

Nation is starting to lose the only thing it had going for it: the Wrigley Field mystique.

19. Harry Caray Dies (1998)

Surprisingly, the broadcaster who became a Cubs institution had lengthy tenures as an announcer with both the St. Louis Cardinals and Chicago White Sox prior to calling games at Wrigley Field. Yet in spite of these prior professional allegiances, Harry Caray was beloved by Cubs fans everywhere almost from the moment he arrived in 1982. He was popular for both his offbeat delivery in the booth and his ubiquity in Chicago's nightlife, particularly in the bars on and around Rush Street. Even as his skills in both areas declined with age (Caray frequently made Yogi Berra–level gaffes during broadcasts), Cubs fans continued to admire him. But it obviously couldn't last forever. Caray died in 1998 of a heart attack. Unlike most of the Cubs' mishaps, setbacks, and tragedies, this one was inevitable. After all, Caray was a mortal man, and he had to go at some point. But deep down, most Cubs fans thought he'd somehow live forever.

20. Lights Installed at Wrigley Field (1988)

For its first seven decades of existence, night games were unheard of at the Friendly Confines. Built for a different era, Wrigley Field was designed for playing baseball on sunny summer afternoons, the way God intended. However, after the Tribune Company bought the team in 1981, it was only a matter of time. The new owners started talking about putting in lights almost immediately, but their efforts were hampered by a couple of very different groups early on. Naturally, the fans were resistant to the idea mainly because it detracted from Wrigley Field's uniqueness. Also, politicians got involved because the park is located smack in the middle of a neighborhood, and huge bright lights might have proved a tad intrusive for the Wrigleyville residents. But the Tribune Company was determined to get those evening dollars. They cajoled, then threatened, and finally offered the decisive ultimatum: give us the lights or we move to the 'burbs. After that, what could Cubs fans say? They certainly couldn't have called the Trib's bluff—otherwise, those drunken preppies and Trixies would be hopping on the Metra to Schaumburg to see games. They just had to accept their team would have a dozen or two night games on the schedule. Still, the baseball gods offered something of a sign to the corporate paymasters who broke with one of the team's grand traditions. The Cubs first-ever night game on August 8, 1988, was rained out after four innings.

21. Cubs Open Season 0–14 (1997)

Every Cubs season since 1909 has brought eventual disappointment with it; the only difference is when the fans are forced to give up hope. Sometimes it's in June. Sometimes the Cubs aren't out of it until August or September. In 1997, however, the die-hards didn't have to wait long to go into "There's Always Next Year" mode. Just a few weeks into April, it was evident that the team wasn't going anywhere that season—in spite of the fact they had a pretty solid lineup that included Sammy Sosa, Ryne Sandberg, and Mark Grace. The team kicked off the year with a 0–14 losing run and finished the first month with a 6–19 record. The culprit? Poor pitching: No team can contend if its most consistent performer on the mound is Kevin Tapani.

22. Sports Illustrated *Picks Cubs to Win World Series (2004)*

You just knew it was a bad sign when *Sports Illustrated* picked the Chicago Cubs to win it all. It was a worse sign that the cover of the April 5 issue featured only Kerry Wood—because Mark Prior was going to begin the season on the disabled list. If the 2004 Cubs needed anything, it wasn't added pressure. They certainly didn't need yet another curse, this time of the *Sports Illustrated* variety. Referred to as the "*SI* Jinx," this phenomenon involves people or teams featured on the cover of an issue. Basically, they end up getting hurt or losing big or [insert negative result here]. Cub Nation had enough to contend with thanks to black cats, goats, and overzealous fans, so when *SI* added its own hex to the mix, along with the headline "Hell Freezes Over," it became too much for the otherwise-talented Cubs squad to bear. Despite coming within five outs of the World Series in 2003, the ballclub didn't even make the playoffs in 2004, collapsing down the stretch in typical North Side fashion.

23. Mark Prior and Kerry Wood Begin Season on DL (2006)

Losing Derrek Lee to injury for much of the season was bad enough for the Cubbies. But the Cubs being the Cubs, that wasn't the only pain the fans would endure in 2006. Adding to their woes was the fact that Mark Prior and Kerry Wood—two key members of the team's five-man starting rotation—began the year on the DL for the second season in a row. It only got worse when they came back: In the month-long period after both pitchers were reactivated, Prior and Wood combined for a grand total of one win. Worst of all is that the two accounted for $15.65 million of the team's nearly $95 million total payroll in 2006.

24. Cubs Trade Dontrelle Willis (2003)

It wasn't quite Lou Brock revisited when the Cubs traded left-handed pitcher Dontrelle Willis to the Florida Marlins for Matt Clement and Antonio Alfonseca in March 2002, but the exchange had profound effects on both ballclubs the very next season. Willis—who looked to be just another ready-to-disappoint Cubs pitching prospect at the time of the trade—went 14–6 with a 3.30 ERA in 2003 and was named the NL Rookie of the Year. That alone would have been enough to warrant regret, but "D-Train" and the Marlins also beat the Cubs in the 2003 NLCS. The Marlins would go on to defeat the New York Yankees in the World Series, while the Cubs went home. Meanwhile, Clement went 9–13 for the Cubs in 2004, then left for the Red Sox, while Antonio Alfonseca had a 5.83 ERA in 2003 and has bounced around the majors ever since.

25. Sammy Sosa Corks Bat (2003)

He may have been corking his muscles with steroids for years, but there was never any proof, so Sammy Sosa's reputation remained relatively untarnished the first 14 seasons of his career. The same cannot be said for season 15, when the prodigious slugger was caught using a corked bat in a game against the Tampa Bay Devil Rays. Rather

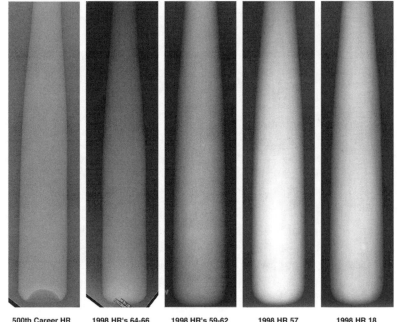

SAMMY SOSA'S HALL OF FAME BATS

| 500th Career HR | 1998 HR's 64-66 | 1998 HR's 59-62 | 1998 HR 57 | 1998 HR 18 |

In the aftermath of Sammy Sosa's corking scandal, all of his bats were sent to the Hall of Fame to be x-rayed. Although no cork was found in any of them, the second one from the left showed traces of salsa on the handle.

than admitting his mistake, however, Sosa amplified Cub Nation's embarrassment, claiming that he used the illegal bat only for batting practice and home-run contests. The defense rang hollow and helped contribute to a falling out between Cubs fans and their once-beloved slugger. In true Cubs fashion, Sosa spent the next season and a half chipping away at his legacy and becoming somewhat of a joke, giving Cubs faithful a whole new reason to feel humiliated. On the upside, the corking incident would eventually take a back seat to Sammy's bizarre injuries, his ballooned ego, and the rampant steroid rumors, which would dog him even after retirement.

26. Cubs Lose to Giants in National League Championship Series (1989)

If only Cubs manager Don Zimmer were taller, maybe things would have gone differently. Maybe San Francisco Giants slugger Will Clark wouldn't have been able to read Greg Maddux mouth the word "fastball" over Zimmer's head and hit that grand slam to seal Game 1. But Clark did hit that grand slam, and another impressive Chicago Cubs season (93–69) went by the board as they fell to the Giants 4–1 in the NLCS. Perhaps the saddest part about the series was Mark Grace's wasted performance: The first baseman hit .647, driving in eight runs. On the other hand, veteran slugger Andre Dawson had just two hits in the series, batting a paltry .105 and driving in three runs. Vaunted pitcher Greg Maddux was 0–1 with a 13.50 ERA. The Boys of Zimmer had been reduced to also-rans. They wouldn't win another division title for 14 years.

27. Jim Riggleman Hired as Cubs Skipper (1995)

After managing the San Diego Padres to a 112–179 record in just over two seasons, Jim Riggleman was hired to become the Chicago Cubs' sixth manager of the '90s. That's right: halfway through the decade, the North Siders were already on skipper number six, and this was the best guy they could find. It proved to be a perfect fit, as he would go on to helm the SS *Cubbie Blue* for five seasons, guiding the club to a record of 374–419. In 1999, Riggleman's last year as manager, he presided over a dismal 26–57 record after the All-Star break. He was summarily fired, and Cubs fans were excited about Riggleman's replacement, Don Baylor, right up until he led the Cubs to a 65–97 record in 2000, somehow besting Riggleman's worst record by two losses.

28. Cubs Collapse in Last Week of Wild-Card Race (2004)

It was the season after "the Season," and the Cubs were finally supposed to win it all. And with the end of the season just over a week away, the Cubs were in position to nab the 2004 NL wild-card. Then came the collapse, in every sense of the word. It wasn't just the losing, although dropping seven of their last nine games wasn't exactly fun. It was also the manner in which they lost: late. LaTroy Hawkins alone gave up more game-losing home runs in the final two weeks than most pitchers do in a lifetime. Sammy Sosa choked. Nomar Garciaparra choked. Just about the only guy who didn't was Prior. On September 30, he went nine innings and struck out 16, only to watch his teammates drop their second-straight 12-inning game. Management also self-destructed down the stretch, blaming WGN broadcaster Steve Stone for the team's troubles. According to some estimates, more than 10,000 fans cried themselves to death on the last day of the season.

29. Cubs Lose to Atlanta Braves in National League Division Series (1998)

North Side fans were given all sorts of false hope going into the 1998 playoffs, buoyed by Kerry Wood's Rookie of the Year performance, along with Sammy Sosa's heroic battle with Mark McGwire for the single-season home-run record. Cub Nation just figured Sosa and Wood would carry the club into the World Series, or at least the NLCS. What happened instead was a total deflation. The Atlanta Braves easily swept the wild-card Cubs, outscoring them 15–4 in three games. Sosa batted .182, going 2–11 with 0 RBIs, and an injured Kerry Wood pitched well in the final game, only to have the bullpen get jacked for five runs in four innings. Wood subsequently underwent Tommy John surgery in the off-season, and he has never been the same since.

30. Cubs Go 11 Seasons without a Winning Record (1973–83)

Seven different men managed the Chicago Cubs from 1973 to 1983, and each proved equally capable of helming a loser. The only season during this stretch the Cubs didn't lose more games than they won was 1977, when the team somehow pulled off a nonembarrassing 81–81 mark. But that minor achievement would be overshadowed by a 704–943 (.427) record in one of the worst dry spells in Cubs history. Combined with Ernie Banks's retirement in 1971 and the end of Leo Durocher's reign as manager in 1972, these years also marked the end of an era: Ron Santo left the Cubs in 1974; Billy Williams in 1975; Randy Hundley retired in 1977; and Fergie Jenkins retired in 1983. The other notable change was the purchasing of the Chicago Cubs by the Tribune Company in 1981 during a strike-shortened year, so the club wouldn't have a chance to celebrate the new ownership until 1982, when they went 79–83.

31. Cubs Produce "Believe" Bracelets (2005)

Always looking for a new expressway to Profit Town, the Chicago Cubs cashed in on a trend in 2005, hopping onto the fashion bandwagon started by Lance Armstrong's yellow "Livestrong" rubber bracelets, which were sold in packs of five and 10 in an effort to raise $5 million for cancer research. The Cubs' goal was equally noble. They wanted to bring in the dollars. The blue "Believe" bracelets were unveiled January 21, 2005, at the 20th annual Cubs Convention. Thousands of attendees gobbled them up for the attractive price of $2 apiece, then quickly turned around and sold them on eBay for between $10 and $20 each. By the start of the 2005 season, 94 percent of all Cubs fans were wearing the blue bracelets, but no amount of manufactured belief would save the ragtag Cubs squad, which finished the season in fourth place with a 79–83 record. While Believe bracelets still exist, they do so mostly in private, hidden in sock drawers.

32. Cubs Lose to Boston Red Sox in World Series (1918)

Despite featuring starting pitchers with names like Hippo, Lefty, and Claude, the Chicago Cubs fell to the Boston Red Sox 4–2 in what would be Boston's final World Series victory for 86 years. The Cubs, meanwhile, were just 10 years into what will likely turn into a century-long championship drought. While North Side fans had no way of knowing what struggles the next nine decades would bring, this Series should have provided some clues, as the Cubs' pitching staff had a combined 1.04 ERA but was only able to eke out two victories. On the bright side, the Cubs were able to hold Babe Ruth to just two RBIs in the Series, but that provided little solace as Ruth went 2–0 on the mound with a 1.06 ERA.

33. Beer Price Tops $4 (2004)

Enough said.

34. Cubs Open Wrigley Field Premium Ticket Services (2003)

What's the only thing worse than waiting in line for Cubs tickets? The Tribune Company answered that question when it established its very own ticket brokerage. Wrigley Field Premium Ticket Services, which bills itself as "the only licensed ticket broker endorsed by the Chicago Cubs," in fact has something of an incestuous relationship with the team. These two kissin' cousins are both owned by the Trib.

Here's how it works. Wrigley Field Premium Ticket Services "purchases" tickets from the Cubs, inflates the prices (often many times over, depending on the game and seat), and then sells them to some sucker, maybe you. There are several problems with this arrangement. First of all, it borders on scalping. Second, buyers pay more in two ways: one on the mark-up from Wrigley Field Premium Ticket Services and another from the City of Chicago's 8 percent amusement tax, which is exacted on the difference between the face value and the ticket broker's resale price. Finally, as others have pointed out, the Tribune Company has found a way to recoup at least some of the expense involved with paying their proportionate percentage of MLB dues from ticket sales via the brokerage. The corporation can sell off blocks of the tickets to another company it owns, which will then resell them at a much higher price but only report their income from face-value ticket revenues to the league each year. There's nothing wrong with this in and of itself, but if the Trib employed the same level of cunning to fielding a great team that it applies in financial matters, the Cubs would be going for their fifth straight World Series title in 2007.

35. Lee Elia Drops F-Bombs on Cubs Fans (1983)

Lee Elia, the Cubs' manager in 1983, was clearly frustrated by the team's slow start, but he was even more aggravated by the fans' very vocal disparagement of the players on the field. In an April 19 postgame press conference, he reached his breaking point. The following is an edited sample:

F——k those f——kin' fans who come out here and say they're Cub fans that are supposed to be behind you rippin' every f——kin' thing you do. I'll tell you one f——kin' thing, I hope we get f——kin' hotter than s——t, just to stuff it up them 3,000 f——kin' people that show up every f——kin' day, because if they're the real Chicago f——kin' fans, they can kiss my f——kin' ass right downtown and *print it.* They're really, really behind you around here...my f——kin' ass. What the f——k am I supposed to do, go out there and let my f——kin' players get destroyed every day and be quiet about it? For the f——kin' nickel-dime people who turn up? The motherf——kers don't even work. That's why they're out at the f——kin' game. They oughtta go out and get a f——kin' job and find out what it's like to go out and earn a f——kin' living. Eighty-five percent of the f——kin' world is working. The other 15 percent comes out here. A f——kin' playground for the c—suckers. Rip them motherf——kers. Rip them f——kin' c—suckers like the f——kin' players.

Now, all of us succumb to the temptation to drop an f-bomb or two every now and then. But Elia's tirade was the verbal equivalent of Hiroshima. Needless to say, it didn't go over well with the Cubs front office or fans, and he was gone by the end of August.

36. Mike Ditka Sings Seventh-Inning Stretch (1998)

For almost all Chicagoans, Mike "Da Coach" Ditka is a legend. He led the Bears to a Super Bowl that is still talked about in Chicago as though it happened last week, he was a key element of one of the most popular and long-running sketches on *Saturday Night Live*, and his restaurant serves the best pork chops in the Windy City, if not the United States. However, his star faded a little bit when he sang "Take Me Out to the Ballgame" during the seventh-inning stretch at Wrigley Field in 1998.

To be fair, this was Ditka, a gruff, cigar-smoking ex-coach with a nasally midwestern accent. No one expected a Pavarotti-esque performance from him. However, his rendition of the song fell even lower than the fans' very low expectations. According to Chip Caray, Ditka was running late because he had played a round of golf earlier that day. When he arrived at Wrigley Field, he flew up the steps and unceremoniously grabbed the microphone, then rushed through the song while out of breath. The result was that Ditka, who sounded like he just had his wisdom teeth taken out, was off key, off beat, off pitch, off everything.

Amazingly, he was asked back five more times.

37. Shawon Dunston's Mediocre Cubs Career (1985–97)

Shawon Dunston never quite lived up to his potential. Oh, sure, he went to two All-Star Games, but this guy was supposed to be special. He was supposed to go to 10 All-Star

Games, win the MVP, and hit .300 every other year. He was also supposed to turn his absolute canon of an arm into a sniper rifle so he could win multiple Gold Gloves. Instead, Dunston's career was a maddening enigma for Cubs fans, who loved the shortstop to death but just couldn't understand why he never figured it out. First, there was his arm. The guy could throw an egg through a brick wall, whatever that means. The only problem was that Dunston often had no idea where his throws were going. If it weren't for Gold Glove first baseman Mark Grace, Dunston's already-high error totals would have been shockingly awful. At the plate, Dunston was as streaky as they get. He inspired the unforgettable "Shawon-O-Meter," poster-board signs that fans held up displaying his average that day in hopes that he would someday reach .300. The signs also featured the words, "And rising...!" but it usually wasn't the case. Despite all the potential, Dunston turned out to be a career .269 hitter.

38. Mitch Williams Busts as Cubs Closer (1990)

The Chicago Cubs caught lightning in a bottle in 1989, when newly acquired closer Mitch Williams had 36 thrilling, volatile saves for the playoff-bound North Siders. Never mind the fact that the Cubs gave up Rafael Palmeiro and Jamie Moyer in the eight-player deal...this seemed like a good trade at the time. But there was always something bad brewing beneath the surface, as his nickname, "Wild Thing," indicated. Despite his 36 saves in 1989, Williams gave up 52 walks in 81.7 innings pitched. The next season this wildness boiled over: Williams surrendered 50 walks in

66.3 innings, had a 1–8 record, and saved only 16 games. His blown saves were a major frustration as the Cubs went 77–85 just one year after they won 93 games. Williams was traded to the Phillies following his brutal 1990 season, and he eventually returned to form in 1993, saving 43 games. But his Cubness didn't leave him for long; in the 1993 World Series he had a 20.25 ERA, blowing two saves and serving up a bottom-of-the-ninth Series-losing home run to Joe Carter.

39. Mark Grace Wins World Series—with Diamondbacks (2001)

While hardly a slugger, Mark Grace was consistent, getting more than 2,500 hits over the course of his 16-year career. He was also a solid fielder, winning four Gold Gloves. However, Grace occasionally clashed with the team's management over his raucous participation in Chicago's nocturnal social scene. Also, there was something of a running feud between him and Sammy Sosa. These issues came to a head in 2000, when the Cubs opted not to renew his contract. After leaving Chicago, he was snatched up by the Arizona Diamondbacks, a team that had gobbled up many talented free agents in the previous few years thanks to big-spending owner Jerry Colangelo. Grace turned out to be one of the team's key contributors that season, with his seminal moment coming in Game 7 of the World Series. Down 2–1 in the ninth inning, he hit a leadoff single against feared Yankees closer Mariano Rivera that commenced his team's game- and Series-winning rally. This play gave the expansion Diamondbacks a World Series victory within their first five years of existence and one more than Grace's former team had managed to win in the previous nine decades.

40. Ryne Sandberg Walks Away (1994)

If it were up to Cubs fans, Ryne Sandberg would play second base at Wrigley Field forever. With the possible exceptions of Ernie Banks and Ron Santo, no Cubs player was more beloved by the fans during his career than the slick-fielding, smooth-swinging Sandberg. Or Ryno, as everybody called him. You never want to see a player like him leave the game prematurely, but that's exactly what Sandberg did on June 13, 1994, when the struggling second baseman retired in the middle of the season. According to Sandberg, in his book *Second to Home*, "The reason I retired is simple: I lost the desire that got me ready to play on an everyday basis for so many years. Without it, I didn't think I could perform at the same level I had in the past, and I didn't want to play at a level less than what was expected of me by my teammates, coaches, ownership, and most of all, myself." It was a crushing blow to Cubs fans, and coupled with the player's strike, which came two months later, 1994 became a season to forget on the North Side.

41. Cubs Lose to New York Yankees in World Series (1932)

You can't really blame the Cubs for losing to the juggernaut 107–47 Yankees squad. It was the way the Cubs lost. Their pitching staff had a combined ERA of 9.26, and the Yankees swept the Cubs 4–0 in a total rout of a Series, but this fall classic will forever be remembered for Babe Ruth's called shot. In the fifth inning of Game 3 at Wrigley Field, Charley Root was on the hill, and Ruth was at the plate with the score tied 4–4. Down two strikes, Ruth gestured toward the bleachers, then crushed the next pitch into the center-field seats. The Yankees won 7–5 and completed the sweep the next day with a 13–6 drubbing of the Cubs. Ruth's called shot would begin an ominous trend of Cubs games being remembered more for achievements by opposing players than for anything the Cubs themselves actually did on the field.

42. Cubs Unveil Precious Moments Giveaway (2002)

One might argue the Chicago Cubs could use as many precious moments as they can get their paws on. But one wouldn't argue that if one were a self-respecting baseball fan. So when the Cubs announced they were giving away miniature ceramic collectibles known as Precious Moments on Mother's Day 2002, it marked a new low in the franchise's promotional history. What ever happened to normal giveaways like baseball cards or beer mugs? The Cubs have enough trouble trying to prove they aren't wimps without distributing sappy figurines to eager fans once a year. But Cub Nation being Cub Nation, the 2002 promotion was a huge success, so every May since, the fans have lined up well before first pitch for the chance to take home a little piece of the Cubs' collective masculinity. Clearly a prelude to pink Cubs attire, the Precious Moments figurine is the bane of every Cubs fan who ever got called a "sissy," "wimp," or "Sally."

43. Todd Hundley Signs with Cubs (2001)

It sure seemed like Todd Hundley would be a great asset for the Cubs when the team signed him to a four-year, $23.5 million contract in 2001. A two-time All-Star catcher with the New York Mets who hit 41 homers in 1996, he was also the son of Cubs catcher Randy "the Rebel" Hundley and thus had some sense of the team's proud tradition. Indeed, the younger Hundley showed that he was intimately familiar with that tradition by absolutely sucking during his two-year stint with the North Siders. When he wasn't on the DL or out drinking his sorrows away at various Wrigleyville pubs, he averaged .187 and .211 at the plate during 2001 and 2002. He had a grand total of 28 home runs and 66 RBIs in those two seasons...combined. By the end of his tenure in Chicago, he had even inspired a website called dumpToddHundley.com. Hundley continued to haunt Wrigleyville after he was traded away in 2003, as the Cubs were still on the hook for a part of his outlandish contract money.

44. Cubs Lose to Detroit Tigers in World Series (1935)

Ten years before the more notable postseason matchup between the Chicago Cubs and the Detroit Tigers, there was this one, which the Cubs lost in six games. Generally forgettable, the 1935 World Series did provide some fireworks in Game 3, when umpire George Moriarty ejected Cubs manager Charlie Grimm and shortstop Billy Jurges in the third inning. The Cubs ended up losing the game 6–5 in extra innings, thanks to an unearned Tiger run in the eleventh. While it's not exactly clear what prompted the ejections, MLB commissioner Judge Landis levied $200 fines to everyone involved after the season: Moriarty, Grimm, Jurges, Woody English, and Billy Herman. The Cubs followed their 100-win season in 1935 with two second-place finishes before winning the pennant in 1938, only to be crushed by the New York Yankees in the World Series.

45. Cubs Lose 100 Games for First Time (1962)

From 1947 to 1961, the Cubs enjoyed exactly zero winning seasons. And just when fans on the North Side thought it couldn't get any worse, the once-proud franchise endured the unthinkable: 103 losses. With a 59–103 record, the 1962 Chicago Cubs established a new low in Wrigleyville. It was a frustrating season for the offense (Ron Santo hit just .227, and a young Lou Brock just .263), but the pitching is what really crushed any chance of success. The staff featured a bloated ERA of 4.54, yielding 159 home runs and 601 bases on balls. Coming on the heels of the failed "College of Coaches" experiment, 1962 provided no relief as the Cubs went through three forgettable managers that aren't even worth mentioning, except one of them, Charlie Metro, because he had a cool name.

46. Cubs Lose 100 Games for Second Time (1966)

Of his 1966 ballclub, first-year manager Leo Durocher said, "Wow, these guys suck." Well, he probably said that, given how horribly the team played en route to its last-place finish and second 59–103 season in just five years. This time around, the pitchers were once again the problem, ranking dead last in the National League in a variety of key areas: ERA, hits, runs, home runs, shutouts, and angry fans shouting, "We need a pitcher, not a belly itcher." Durocher would eventually pull it together and prove to be a decent manager, but only until 1969, when the extremely talented Cubs self-destructed during a pennant race with the New York Mets.

47. Sammy Sosa Hit in Head by Pitch (2003)

Just one plate appearance after tying Eddie Murray for 17th place on Major League Baseball's all-time home-run list, Sammy Sosa stepped into the batter's box against Pittsburgh Pirates hurler and fellow Dominican Republic native Salomon Torres. Arguably, it would be the last time in Sosa's career he would feel comfortable at the plate, because the pitch Torres threw was a 90-plus-mph fastball directly at Sosa's head. The ball connected with Sosa's left temple, smashing his helmet and leaving the Cubs slugger dazed and upset. While he escaped the incident without major injury, the mental toll from the horrific beaning would ultimately lead to the twilight of Sosa's career. A mere two months later, a struggling Sammy was caught using a corked bat in an effort to reignite his stagnant swing. The beaning also prompted him to stand much farther from the plate, making him susceptible to outside strikes and all but eliminating his opposite-field power.

48. Joe Carter Hired as Cubs Broadcaster (2001)

It would be tough for anyone to replace Steve Stone in the Cubs broadcast booth, but that doesn't mean anyone couldn't have done a better job than Joe Carter. When Stone left as WGN's color commentator (the first time), the geniuses in the Tribune Tower knew they had to pull in a heavy hitter. Unfortunately, they weren't able to do that, so Hall of Fame slugger Joe Carter would have to do. It's important to mention Carter's Hall of Fame standing, as he often used tales of his playing days as a crutch whenever he couldn't think of something to say about the actual game being played right in front of his eyes. While there's no way to verify the exact number, it's estimated that Carter casually mentioned his World Series–winning home run off Mitch Williams approximately 3,000 times during his two-year stint in the WGN booth. He also failed to build a rapport with play-by-play man Chip Caray, other than to step over his partner's words a few times a minute. Carter was not particularly gifted in grammar or math, often leading to gaffes combining his two weaknesses, such as the time he said, "Kerry Wood's fastball takes less time to get to the plate, so hitters has more time to react."

49. Jerome Walton's Sophomore Slump (1990)

Unlike many Cubs prospects, Jerome Walton actually lived up to the hype. At least for a few months. The year was 1989, and the Chicago Cubs were playing well. Walton, their young center fielder, looked to have a bright future in the big leagues. He had a decent bat, good speed, and was an above-average outfielder. But it was his remarkable 30-game hitting streak that catapulted him into the national spotlight, earning him the National League Rookie of the Year Award. Cubs fans couldn't help themselves when it came to expecting a long All-Star-studded career from Walton. What should have concerned them was that Walton hit .338 during his streak, the lowest recorded batting average for any 30-game hitting streak in Major League history (20 of the 30 games were single-hit performances). Outside the streak, Walton hit a pedestrian .274. Which is better than the .263 average he put up in 1990 as he regressed into a pronounced sophomore slump. The bloom was off the rose as Walton had just 21 RBIs and was 14–21 in stolen base attempts. His glove slumped, too: he went from a .990 fielding percentage with three errors in 1989 to a .977 fielding percentage with six errors in 1990. Despite Walton's stellar rookie performance, he spent just a few years as a Cub, and his career petered out over the course of 10 seasons with five teams. His second-longest hit streak was like six or seven games, probably.

50. Cubs Give Up on Corey Patterson (2006)

When the Cubs used the third overall pick in the 1998 draft to select an 18-year-old Corey Patterson straight out of high school, the team was sure the decision would change the franchise forever. Hailed as a "five-tool" player, Patterson was supposed to blossom into the next Lou Brock (the one the Cubs wouldn't trade) and be a cornerstone of the

Corey Patterson, shown after striking out with the bases loaded for the second time in a 5–3 loss in 2004, is widely regarded as the most overhyped Cub ever.

organization. Just a few years later, Cubs brass couldn't wait any longer, so they rushed Patterson to the big leagues. The inexperienced center fielder struggled mightily, striking out with alarming frequency and drawing just 28 walks in his first 793 at-bats. Not exactly the type of numbers you want from a five-tool speedster. After a successful first half in 2003, Patterson suffered a season-ending knee injury. He regressed in 2004 and 2005, batting .245 in his final two seasons as a Cub. He was traded to the Baltimore Orioles in January 2006 for two minor leaguers and is generally considered the most overhyped player in Cubs history. But the Cubs being the Cubs, they learned nothing: Eric Patterson, Corey's younger brother, is currently in the Cubs' farm system.

51. Bleacher Tickets Become Outrageously Priced (Ongoing)

There was a time when you could buy a bleacher ticket for $4. That time was not 1960, 1970, or even 1980. It was 1987. Since then, prices have steadily increased, easily outpacing the rate of inflation. In 2006, the total cost for a bleacher ticket (including taxes and "convenience charges") ranged from $35 to $47 per game. But that's not really the price, because odds are you can't get bleacher tickets at face value from the Cubs official ticket office. Odds are the scalpers got them first, or Wrigley Field Premium Ticket Services gobbled them up and will now sell them to you for $60 to $200 per ticket, depending on the game. So why the jump in prices? It's not like the club has become some sort of division-winning juggernaut.

The answer, as is always the case, is much simpler: the Tribune Company knows the fans will pay the price, no matter how high it goes. Thanks in large part to night games, the Wrigley Field bleachers have been transformed into a giant singles party.

52. Cubs Lose to Philadelphia Athletics in World Series (1910)

Just two years into what would become the longest championship drought in major sports history, player/manager Frank Chance led the Cubs to a stellar 104–50 record in the regular season and a date with the Philadelphia Athletics in the World Series. Alas, it was not meant to be, as the Cubs were nearly swept away in a 4–1 Series rout, with the Cubs' only victory coming in Game 4 after 10 innings and three Athletics errors. Adding insult to injury, Philadelphia needed only two pitchers in the entire series—durable righties Jack Coombs and Chief Bender combined for a 2.76 ERA in a whopping 45.7 innings pitched—while the Cubs ran out seven hurlers of their own but were still outscored 35–15 in five games.

53. Ryne Sandberg Comes Back (1996)

To the delight of most Cubs fans, Ryne Sandberg's "retirement" barely lasted longer than a year, and he was on the field again at the start of the 1996 season. It started well enough: his first hit in a regular-season game was a home run off Pedro Astacio. And he had a decent year all around, with 25 home runs, 92 RBIs, and 82 double plays. Still, Sandberg would not be like Moses leading the Chicago

Cubs to the promised land, as so many of the team's supporters had hoped. Really, Ryno's comeback did little more than pad his own stats (he finished with 277 homers, the most ever for a second baseman at the time) and promote his bid for the Hall of Fame. He retired again for good the following year, with Chicago finishing below .500 in both 1996 and 1997.

54. Leon Durham's Error in National League Championship Series (1984)

Leon Durham had a good seven-plus-season career with the Cubs and was a key member of the team that went to the NLCS in 1984. Alas, his most significant contribution that year was a huge negative for the team, and one that's earned him eternal ire in the hearts of Cubs fans. It was the sixth inning of the decisive Game 5, and things were looking good for the Cubs. The team led 3–0, but a pair of sacrifice flies in the bottom of the inning drove in a couple of runs for the Padres. The next inning, a visibly tired Rick Sutcliffe walked Carmelo Martinez, who advanced to second on a Garry Templeton sacrifice fly. Next up was Tim Flannery, who ripped a grounder toward first base. Durham attempted to field the hit, but it went through his legs like a croquet ball through a wicket, and Martinez plated. To be fair, the game was only tied 3–3 at that point, and the Cubs allowed three more runs in a 6–3 Padres victory. And Durham's overall numbers that year suggest he was a key factor in their playoff run. But Cubs fans will always remember him as, "That asshole who ruined '84."

55. Mike Harkey Injured Doing Cartwheel for Bleacher Chicks (1992)

Pitching prospect Mike Harkey was drafted in 1984 by San Diego, but he decided not to sign with the team, something that Padres management must have been happy about in hindsight. Of course, when he reentered the draft three years later, the Cubs were only too happy to pick him up. In a few ways, Harkey was the quintessential Cubs player. For example, he only won 26 games in the five seasons he played in Chicago, about five per year. Also, he was on the DL a lot. One of the most memorable injuries for Harkey came early in 1992 as a result of a little hot-dogging. In an effort to impress some babes in the stands, Harkey turned a cartwheel on the field in front of them during batting practice. While he can't be faulted for relying on this time-honored pick-up technique—if you ever want to impress a girl at a bar, simply turn a cartwheel in front of her—it backfired when it led to a season-ending injury. The Cubs let him go the following year, but for some reason, he wound up playing for two more teams at the major-league level after pulling this failed gymnastics stunt.

56. Dusty Baker Doesn't Get It Done, Man (2003–06)

When Dusty Baker was named Cubs manager in November 2002, Wrigleyville finally had reason to believe. Not only did Baker have a reputation as a cool customer, but he was also a three-time NL Manager of the Year coming off a season in which he led the San Francisco

Giants to the World Series. They didn't win it, but so what? The 2002 Cubs could barely dream of getting to the fall classic, let alone actually winning it. And then, in 2003, it almost happened. Thanks in large part to aces Mark Prior and Kerry Wood, Baker and the Cubs shocked the world by going 88–74. They won the NL Central and nearly marched to the World Series—only to collapse in Game 6 of the NLCS against the Florida Marlins. Still, despite the disappointment of being only five outs away from the Promised Land (and then not making it), Baker had ushered in a new era of Cubs dominance. Only...he hadn't. Baker led the Cubs on a steady decline over the next three years, with the North Siders ultimately losing a whopping 96 games in 2006, good for last place in the National League. Even the magical 2003 can't change the fact that Dusty Baker's reign will go down in the annals of Cubdom as yet another unmitigated disaster.

57. Will Clark Reads Greg Maddux's Lips Before Grand Slam (1989)

At the Republican National Convention in 1988, then-candidate George Bush made the famous proclamation: "Read my lips: no new taxes!" Of course, nearly everyone who read his lips was pretty peeved a few years later when President Bush broke his word and raised taxes. A year after the RNC, another lip-reading situation would garner headlines, this time in the world of sports. In Game 1 of the 1989 National League Championship Series, slugger Will "the Thrill" Clark faced Cubs ace Greg Maddux in the latter's first postgame outing. Maddux's inexperience showed: Clark bloodied his nose early when he drove in two runs with a double in the first inning, then hit a solo homer in the third. He wasn't done yet, though. Facing Maddux in the fourth, Clark stood and watched as manager Don Zimmer came out to the mound for a chat with his green pitcher. Clark later confessed he saw Maddux say "fastball in" during this discussion. Unlike Bush, Maddux delivered exactly what he said he would. Knowing what was coming, the Thrill nailed the pitch for a grand slam that gave the Giants a 7–3 lead on their way to an 11–3 rout of the Cubs that set the tone for the series. And Maddux? He now covers his mouth with his glove whenever he converses with anyone on the mound.

58. Steve Stone Gets Bitter, Then Steps Down (2004)

Following a solid, 11-season pitching career, Steve Stone stepped into the broadcast booth for Tribune-owned WGN television in 1983. He joined legendary announcer Harry Caray, and Stone's insightful commentary proved to be a great complement to the entertaining malapropisms of his senior partner. After Harry Caray's death in early 1998, his grandson Chip joined Stone in the booth. While no one could replace Caray (not even his descendant), Stone and Caray III meshed well. Health problems sidelined Stone between 2001 and 2002, but he came back in time for the Cubs' playoff run—and epic collapse—in 2003. Stone returned to the booth the following year a changed man. He was much more critical in his comments, particularly where Dusty Baker's management style was concerned. Moreover, Cubs pitcher Kent Mercker heckled Stone right back for what he perceived to be unfair disparagements of the team. (The idea of Stone, who won the Cy Young Award and achieved a 25-win season, being jeered by the middling Mercker, the Ford Taurus of pitchers, is nauseatingly amusing.) All of this got to be too much for Stone, who stepped down at the end of the 2004 season. In spite of his withering critiques of the team, he remained popular with fans until the very end—probably because they realized the Cubs deserved so much worse than what Stone dished out.

59. Tinker, Evers, and Chance Infield Broken Up (1911–13)

Not many teams in baseball history truly deserve to be called dominant in a given era. Cincinnati's Big Red Machine of the early to mid-1970s certainly qualifies, as does just about any Yankees squad from the late '20s through the late '50s. Believe it or not, the Chicago Cubs once had a dominant team as well. At the core of this collection of world-beaters was an incredible infield comprised of future Hall of Famers Joe Tinker at shortstop, Johnny Evers at second, and Frank Chance at first (as well as third baseman Harry Steinfeldt, to a lesser extent). These guys played together with few respites from 1903 to 1910.

How good were they? The Cubs won four pennants and two World Series during that span. In addition, the team got 116 wins in a 154-game season, a record that still stands today. (The Seattle Mariners tied this total in 2001, but they played 162 games that year.) Tinker, Evers, and Chance even inspired a poem that was famous in its day. It was penned by nationally known news columnist Franklin Pierce Adams, who titled it "Tinker to Evers to Chance."

However, there were problems off the field. Although they became friends many decades later, Tinker and Evers despised one another during their playing days, and the latter had a nervous breakdown in 1911 that shut him down that season. That same year, Chance got plunked with a pitch that nearly killed him. The dissolution was complete by 1913, when Chance went to New York to manage the Yankees and Tinker took over as manager for the Cincinnati Reds.

60. Red Sox Win World Series (2004)

One of the things that made the Cubs' cursed-by-fate status tolerable was the fact that there was another storied, prestigious organization out there that also couldn't win it all: the Boston Red Sox. In fact, the Red Sox's curse actually seemed worse. While the Cubs' hex involved a barnyard animal, Boston's torment was the result of having dealt away Babe Ruth, the best baseball player ever. In 1920 Red Sox owner Harry Frazee traded the Babe to the New York Yankees (back then an ally of Boston, along with the Chicago White Sox) for cash in order to purchase Fenway Park, which he didn't own at the time. He actually traded a few more stars to the Yanks that year, too, to put his proverbial thumb in the eye of American League president and antagonist Ban Johnson and the "Loyal Five" clubs aligned with him. Of course, the popular narrative goes that Frazee sold the Babe to finance an asinine Broadway theatrical production called *No, No, Nanette*, which is what the Curse of the Bambino was based on. That's right, it was all a lie.

Yet the "curse" enjoyed a good run and helped explain the Red Sox's 80-plus years of failure to win the World Series in the minds of both the team's fans and followers of baseball. This was reinforced by incidents like Bill Buckner's infamous error in Game 6 of the 1986 World Series. However, the jig was up in 2004, when Kevin Millar, Johnny Damon, David Ortiz, Curt Shilling, and the other "cowboys" completely reversed the momentum in an amazing ALCS against the now-hated Yankees, then swept the St. Louis Cardinals in the World Series. The jig was up for the Cubs, too, who couldn't rely on their scapegoat the way they had before. Plus, now they were completely alone in their loserdom. (Unless they counted the White Sox, which, being Cubs fans, they didn't.)

61. LaTroy Hawkins (2004–05)

When the Cubs signed former Minnesota Twins reliever LaTroy Hawkins in December 2003, they were getting the best setup man in baseball. But when Cubs closer Joe Borowski went down with an injury in early 2004, Hawkins was forced to change roles and become the worst closer in the majors. It was a role in which Hawkins would thrive. Despite his respectable 2.63 ERA, the righty struggled all season long, converting just 25 of 34 save opportunities. He was particularly adept at blowing one-run-save chances. The fans at Wrigley Field commended Hawkins for his poor play by booing him periodically throughout the year. But it was the final two weeks of 2004 that cemented the fans' hatred for Hawkins. He blew every save opportunity down the stretch in excruciating fashion as the Cubs went 2–7 in their last nine games of the season. Hawkins was not solely responsible for the collapse, but he was certainly the biggest part of it. In 2005 the Cubs were forced to trade Hawkins to the San Francisco Giants after the combustible closer blew four of his first eight save opportunities. The deal ended one of the ugliest fan-player relationships in Chicago Cubs history.

62. Grant DePorter Blows Up Bartman Ball (2004)

How do you exorcise the demons of the Cubs' cursed 2003 National League Championship Series? Why, blow up the ball used during the play that may or may not have anything to do with the team's loss, of course. That's the conclusion that Grant DePorter came to, anyway. DePorter, the Chicago restaurateur who owns—among other establishments—Harry Caray's Restaurant, apparently decided that the ball had absorbed all the Cubs' bad juju when Bartman made his fateful grab in Game 6 of the NLCS against the Florida Marlins. Thus it had to be destroyed. First DePorter had to get it. To that end he spent $113,824.16. Then he hired a Hollywood special-effects professional to detonate the ball in a much-ballyhooed, nationally televised ceremony outside of Harry Caray's Restaurant. It was even given a "last meal" of steak and lobster. It turned out to be a terrible investment. Oh sure, the stunt generated lots of publicity for the restaurant. And it raised significant proceeds for diabetes sufferers. However, in terms of alleviating the Cubs' curse, it was probably the worst $113,824 plus change ever spent.

63. Cubs Acquire Pitcher Ernie Broglio (1964)

When the Cubs traded outfielder Lou Brock to the St. Louis Cardinals for pitcher Ernie Broglio in 1964, it seemed like a very good deal. The Cubs were getting rid of someone who hadn't performed well by anyone's standards, and they were getting an ace who had pitched a 21-win season with the Cards and gotten 18 victories the year before the trade. However, something clicked in Brock when he went to St. Louis. He helped lead the team to the World Series championship that same year and did the same in 1967 as an All-Star. And Broglio? He had a 4–7 record and 4.04 ERA with the Cubs during the remainder of the 1964 season. Sadly, that would actually be his best year with the team. Throughout 1965 and 1966, Broglio won a grand total of three games and dropped 12. The Cubs released him after that. "Brock for Broglio" is emblematic for Cubs followers today because it demonstrates the other aspect of the curse: not the part that causes the team to melt down late in the regular season or in the playoffs, but rather the part that makes the Cubs' seemingly sensible trades look ridiculous in retrospect. Also, it makes the Cubs' "loser" status glaringly obvious, as players who don't perform while on the team go on to have great careers—often including an elusive World Series victory—after they're traded.

64. *Film* Rookie of the Year *Released (1993)*

The Cubs' World Series hopes were put off for at least another century with the release of *Rookie of the Year*, a schmaltzy, contrived film about a boy who becomes a pitcher for the North Siders and leads them to...a division title. The plot goes something like this: 13-year-old Henry Rowengartner breaks his arm, but it heals exceptionally well. He finds out just how well while attending a Cubs game. When he catches a home run in the bleachers, he throws it back—to home plate. Needless to say, the team immediately signs this promising young prospect as a reliever. With Chet Steadman (played by a not-yet-psychotic Gary Busey) as a guide, young Henry manages to register save after save through that season, all while navigating the difficulties of fame, fortune, and scheming agents. Of course, there's the climactic showdown near the end of the movie where Henry must win the most important game of his life. Naturally, he does, but it's not Game 7 of the World Series, nor is it even a regular playoff game. It's actually the finale of the regular season, which simply gives the Cubs the NL Central title. (Hey, that's still a pretty good year.) But Henry decides he can't take all the pressure and attention anymore, plus he trips on a baseball in that last game and loses his 100-mph fastball when he falls on his arm. Thus, he goes back to his regular life of Little League baseball. The kicker, though, is the deus ex machina at the very end, which shows a Cubs World Series Championship ring on his finger. Accept it, Cubs fans: This is as close as you're going to get to a World Series win for a long time.

65. Cubs Sign Mel Rojas (1997)

For fans who remembered Ernie Broglio, the Cubs' acquisition of reliever Mel Rojas must have seemed like a really bad instance of déjà vu: A hot-shot, sure-thing pitcher comes onto the roster, then immediately collapses in epic fashion. In the case of Rojas, the Cubs were getting a pitcher who had thrown 36 saves the previous season for the now-defunct Montreal Expos. He was going to be a surefire asset for the team. At least the Cubs paid him like he would be: Rojas received $4,583,333 in his first year with the team, a sum second only to the salary of Sammy Sosa. He earned more than Cubs stars like Mark Grace and Ryne Sandberg. The term "earned" is used loosely here, though. Rojas blew save after save for the team in his first month as the Cubs' closer. In fact, they dropped their first 14 contests; their first win came in the second game of a doubleheader against the New York Mets on April 20. They would go on to lose 19 that month. Suffice it to say, Rojas only stayed in Chicago for half a season. But the damage was done. Even though the team had a couple of strong runs later in the year, by that point they were a nonfactor in the playoff race: the Cubs finished fifth in their division at 68–94.

66. Cubs Replace Don Baylor with Bruce Kimm (2002)

It's hard to believe in hindsight, but Cubs fans were actually excited about the 2002 season. In the previous year, the team had finished third in the NL Central with a winning record, and baseball pundits and buffs alike were expecting big things from them in '02. Yet the Cubs stumbled out of spring training and into a very lackluster regular season. Most blamed the Cubs' stumbling start on manager Don Baylor, who many felt had affected the team's chemistry with some controversial personnel moves the year before. With a 5–1 loss to the Atlanta Braves on July 4, 2002—just before the All-Star break—the Cubs fell to 34–49. Baylor was canned the very next day. This move was understandable.

What was not understandable was management's choice to replace him: Bruce Kimm, then skipper of the Cubs' Triple-A affiliate in Iowa. Giving one of the most coveted and demanding manager positions in baseball to a largely unproven minor-leaguer defied logic, unless the Tribune Company had written the season off by that point (a definite possibility). In any case, it sucked for the fans: the only thing more depressing than having to fire a losing manager is hiring another losing manager, and Kimm was definitely a loser. The Cubs went 33–45 during Kimm's tenure and finished fifth in their division with a 67–95 record. He didn't even last the rest of the season. The announcement of his exit went out before the final game of the year, along with news of his replacement: Dusty Baker.

67. Team Uses Cell Phones to Call Bullpen (2006)

One of the things fans visiting Wrigley Field can expect to see are attendees—usually clad in the latest Abercrombie & Fitch clothing line—yapping away on cell phones. What they might not expect to witness is the Cubs managers talking on cellies. Yet this is exactly what happened last season. Apparently taking a cue from the fashion plates up in the bleachers, Cubs manager Dusty Baker began using a cell phone to send instructions out to the bullpen, which is little more than 100 feet away from the dugout in Wrigley Field. Exactly why the team decided to switch to cell phones when the regular landline or even hand signals would suffice isn't known for sure. What is clear is that this is completely unnecessary. The White Sox don't even use cell phones in the dugout, and they play at U.S. Cellular Field.

68. Wrigley Field Starts Falling Apart (2004)

One of the most venerable venues in all of sports, Wrigley Field is more of a draw than the team that plays there. So when the Friendly Confines started to crumble in the summer of 2004, true baseball fans everywhere (except those on Chicago's South Side, perhaps) were upset. On a couple of different occasions within the span of a month, concrete debris fell on or near attendees. The first instance involved an elderly woman getting hit in the foot with a brick-sized chunk that collapsed from the upper deck. Following this incident, another piece fell inches away from a man and his five-year-old son. Understandably, people began to worry. Of course, no one was more worried than Chicago mayor Richard M. Daley. A lifelong White Sox fan from Bridgeport, Illinois, Daley threatened to shut down Wrigley Field if the Cubs owners didn't repair the stadium immediately. They fixed it shortly thereafter to the tune of $2 million, which should have been the end of it. But the city of Chicago fined the Cubs

$6,725 for not having the proper permits, then charged the team $36,010 for retroactive permits for the renovations. This episode served as a lesson of sorts for the team's followers. Fans who insist that Chicago is a Cubs town were reminded that the 800-pound gorilla in city hall doesn't see it that way.

69. Bleachers Renamed Bud Light Bleachers (2006)

The presence of blatant marketing at Wrigley Field is a relatively recent phenomenon, and perhaps no better example of this trend is the "Bud Light" prefix on the hallowed outfield bleachers. Game attendees who come in the famous entrance at the intersection of Sheffield and Waveland Avenues are now greeted by a sign that reads "Bud Light Bleachers." This is an affront to Cubs fans for a couple of reasons, the most important of which is the fact that Bud Light is a product of Anheuser-Busch, the same corporation that has its name plastered on the stadium where the rival St. Louis Cardinals play. Given these circumstances, Cubs fans might expect that Anheuser-Busch had to plead with and throw boatloads of money at the Tribune Company for these naming rights. They'd be right on the second count, but wrong on the first. "The Cubs approached us with this opportunity, and it seemed to us a unique way to improve our presence in Chicago," Anheuser-Busch's vice president of global media and sports marketing Tony Ponturo said of the deal. According to Ponturo, the "Bud Light Bleachers" cost just under $1 million a year.

70. Village People Release "YMCA" (1978)

Back in the late 1970s, a group called the Village People, whose shtick was dressing up as masculine American stereotypes, put out a disco song that covertly explained how homosexual males could meet up at the YMCA to "hang out with all the boys." Not that there's anything wrong with that. For some reason, though, the Cubs decided this would be a great song to play during the seventh-inning stretch. Perhaps it's because it's a catchy pop tune, or maybe it's an homage to the rainbow-bedecked Boys Town area in the nearby neighborhood of Lakeview (which actually has a YMCA). Whatever the reason, the song caught on at Wrigley Field, where fans do the famous dance that accompanies it. Even the beer guys get into it. Yet it's just fuel for the fire for South Siders, who don "Wrigley Field: Home of the World's Largest Gay Bar" T-shirts at every White Sox game.

71. Van Halen Releases "Jump" (1984)

The distinctive synthesizer sounds and sonic screams of lead singer David Lee Roth made "Jump" a radio hit for Van Halen in 1984. That was also the year the Chicago Cubs started playing the song on the ballpark organ during pregame introductions. For the next two decades, Cubs players would run out onto Wrigley Field with this ditty as a musical backdrop. In 2006 "Jump" was played significantly less, as the team decided to go with a handful of songs in a rotation format, but fans at Cubs games can still catch it fairly frequently. The decision to hold on to this song for as long as they did is somewhat strange. It definitely lacks the hard, kick-ass edge of, say, "Thunderstruck" by AC/DC (the pregame anthem for the White Sox). Plus, while it's an undeniably appealing power pop-rock anthem, "Jump" isn't a particularly great motivational device. In fact, the lyrics were inspired by a suicide attempt from a building ledge.

72. Jeff Gordon Sings Seventh-Inning Stretch (2005)

"Rainbow Warrior" Jeff Gordon is one of the most hated men in NASCAR. He made himself extremely disliked in yet another sport when he came to Chicago's North Side in 2005 to sing "Take Me Out to the Ballgame" during the seventh-inning stretch. Before he started singing, Gordon greeted the fans by stating how happy he was to be at "Wrigley Stadium." From then on, it was boos aplenty. As Gordon progressed through the song, he began to slip up on the lyrics, which made the fans jeer and heckle him even more. In all likelihood, he'd never encountered such a negative reaction to a performance, even among his most bitter antagonists at Daytona Arena...err, Daytona International Speedway.

73. Ozzy Osbourne Mumbles Seventh-Inning Stretch (2003)

Back in the 1960s and 1970s, Black Sabbath front man Ozzy Osbourne could really belt out some monster tracks. Few rock stars before or since could wail like he did in songs like "Iron Man," "Sweet Leaf," and "Crazy Train." The man who showed up at Wrigley Field in 2003 was a far cry from that

Ozzy Osbourne's rendition of "Take Me Out to the Ballgame" was the weirdest to date, but he still got a group hug.

heavy metal icon. Ozzy came into the booth with Chip Caray and Steve Stone to sing but proceeded to mutter his way through what might have been lyrics. Only about half of the tune seemed to have been sung in any language at all, much less English. Ozzy certainly provided Cubs fans with the most peculiar version of the song they've ever received, if not the absolute worst (*see*: Jeff Gordon). However, Caray said it was one of the best experiences he had with a guest singer: "As everyone just stands back in shock, he says to every member of our crew that was in the booth—the cameraman, the lighting people, Steve, me, our production assistant—'Thank you very much. My wife and I had a lovely time. Give me a hug.'"

74. Cubs Suffer First Sub-.500 Season Since 1908 (1915)

The 1915 Chicago Cubs went 73–80, which put them in fourth place (out of eight teams) in the National League. It marked the first time since the 1908 World Series that the club had failed to win more games than it lost. In many ways, it was the birth of a new, more inconsistent Cubs franchise. Suddenly losing seasons started to outnumber winning ones, and the postseason failures began to add up. This instability spread to the dugout, where managers were changed like underwear. Nineteen fifteen was Roger Bresnahan's first and only year as Cubs skipper, but this would prove to be perfectly normal in this era. From 1912 to 1917, the Cubs went through six different managers: Frank Chance, Johnny Evers, Hank O'Day, Bresnahan, Joe Tinker, and Fred Mitchell. The low point of the season came when the Brooklyn Dodgers beat the Cubs 13–0 and George Cutshaw went 66 at the plate, tying a record not achieved in 14 years. This was also the last season the Cubs would play at West Side Grounds. In 1916 the club's home games were played in what would eventually become Wrigley Field, a stadium that has never seen a World Series victory—by the home team, anyway.

75. Kevin Orie: Yet Another Third-Base Bust (2002)

With 98 different Cubs third basemen between the Ron Santo and Aramis Ramirez eras, we could focus on any number of busts, but Kevin Orie stands out as a guy who should have succeeded. His numbers were respectable in 1997, his rookie season: a .275 batting average, five triples, and 44 RBIs in just 114 games. But things fell apart the very next year. Orie was dreadful at the plate in 1998, hitting just .181 in 64 games. The Cubs traded him to the Florida Marlins in the middle of the season, and he sucked there, too. In 2002 Orie tried to return to the Cubs after a few years out of the big leagues, but it was not to be. He retired with a .249 average in only 316 career games.

76. Neifi Perez Given Two-Year Contract (2006)

Baseball contracts have become somewhat of a joke ever since Alex Rodriguez was handed a quarter of a billion dollars by the Texas Rangers in 2001. Suddenly everyone was making the big bucks, even ineffective middle relievers. But over the last 10 years, there has been no bigger show of GM idiocy than when Jim Hendry signed utility man Neifi Perez to a two-year, $5 million contract for 2006–07. The first problem was the money: $5 million for an aging backup infielder with no power and a penchant for popping the ball up every other at-bat? The second—and more fundamental—slap in the face to Cubs fans is the fact the Cubs signed Perez for two years. The whole point of a multiyear contract is to lock up a player so you don't have to compete with other teams to re-sign him. Other than a local softball team or two, who the hell is going to be interested in a subpar, 34-year-old pine rider with a weak bat and fading defensive skills? The only saving grace here is that Perez was traded to the Detroit Tigers halfway through his contract for a minor league catcher.

77. Dennis Eckersley Becomes a Great Closer (1987)

With Oakland, of course. Following a three-year stint as a Cubs starting pitcher, during which he compiled a pedestrian 27–26 record with a 4.31 ERA, Dennis Eckersley was traded to the Oakland Athletics for three minor leaguers. Those guys never quite panned out. Eckersley, on the other hand, became one of baseball's premier closers, helping his team get to the World Series in 1988 and win it in 1989. He hadn't won a single award as a Cub, but after he was traded, Eckersley's accomplishments were many: an MVP, a Cy Young Award, two Rolaids Relief Man Awards, ALCS MVP, and *The Sporting News* Pitcher of the Year. The handling of Eckersley is just another example of the Cubs' inability to utilize talent. By the time he became a Cub, the bloom was off Eckersley's rose as a starter, yet the Cubs kept running him out there, not even considering a move to the bullpen, where he would eventually flourish and play his way into the Hall of Fame.

78. Cubs Fan Steals Chad Kreuter's Hat (2000)

If Cubs fans have one thing going for them, it's their reputation as a happy lot. They're fans of baseball's "Lovable Losers," after all, so they are supposed to be lovable, too. This started to change in the late 1990s as ticket prices went up, beer sales skyrocketed, and fans became much more interested in winning (even though the team wasn't). The new wave of drunkenness and anger boiled over on May 16, 2000, in a game against the Los Angeles Dodgers, when a fan sitting near the visitor's bullpen stole reliever Chad Kreuter's hat. Kreuter and several teammates went into the stands to retrieve the hat, and a nine-minute mêlée ensued—as the rest of Wrigley Field cheered it on. It was a sad turning point for Cub Nation. This was the kind of violence that occurred across town at U.S. Cellular Field, not the Friendly Confines. Coupled with a disturbing new trend of throwing objects onto the field to show disapproval, the hat incident helped chip away at the positive image of the Wrigley Field faithful. Instead of happy-go-lucky, some people started seeing Cubs fans as angry and disenchanted.

79. Cubs Block Rooftops with Wind Screens (2002)

The Tribune Company might have a reputation for being greedy, but it sure doesn't act like it. No matter what dollar-grabbing stunt they pull, the good folks at the Trib always come up with a sensible explanation. Such was the case in 2002, when they installed "wind screens" on the fence lining Wrigley Field's bleachers. According to the Tribune Tower, the fans needed protection from the elements. Never mind the fact that bleacher bums have been surviving the wind for decades without incident. Also never mind the fact the Cubs were in the middle of a dispute with local rooftop owners when they decided to put up the "wind screens," which conveniently blocked the view of Wrigley Field from the buildings across the street. According to the Tribune Company, the rooftop owners were getting a free product they weren't entitled to—Chicago Cubs baseball—and that was hurting everybody. Turns out everybody is the same group of people who knew what the Cubs were really up to: squeezing more cash out of a subpar baseball team. In the end, the rooftop owners ponied up about $2 million per season, and the wind problem at Wrigley suddenly went away, along with the screens.

80. The Virtual Waiting Room (2004)

As if purchasing Cubs tickets wasn't painful enough in the pre-technology era, the Cubs took things a step further with the "Virtual Waiting Room" in February 2004. A white rectangle that occupies your computer screen and repeatedly counts backward from 30 to 0, the Virtual Waiting Room is supposed to be where you wait for your chance to buy individual game tickets for the upcoming Cubs season. A more appropriate name would be the Virtual Torture Room because nothing on this earth is more excruciating than waiting *to be allowed* to buy a Cubs bleacher ticket for nearly $50. Especially when it takes three to four hours per purchase, if you're lucky enough to get into the actual system at all. And the odds are you won't get past the Virtual Waiting Room until late afternoon, which means the only tickets left will be for the nosebleed section on a frigid April day game against the Pittsburgh Pirates.

But it's not all bad. There is, surprisingly, hope. When the gods created the awesome frustration force that is the Chicago Cubs, they didn't account for computer geeks, who quickly figured out that you can press Control N (Option N on a Mac) to open as many windows as your screen allows. Instead of waiting like a chump in one Virtual Waiting Room, you could be waiting like a chump in 80 or 90 of them.

81. Nomar Garciaparra Fails as a Cub (2005)

The 2004 trade deadline seemingly had passed without the Cubs making a significant move to upgrade the club that had come within five outs of the World Series in 2003, but then news came of "the Trade." It was a four-team deal between the Cubs, Red Sox, Twins, and Expos. The result was Nomar Garciaparra in a Cubs uniform for at least two years. Everyone figured Cubs GM Jim Hendry had struck gold—just like he did with Aramis Ramirez in 2003. After all, Garciaparra was a two-time American League batting champion and a five-time All-Star short-stop. Unfortunately, in becoming a Cub, the former Red Sox standout was forced to trade in his talent for a string of injuries. He played just 43 games over two months for the 2004 Cubs, hitting a respectable .297 but knocking in just 20 runs. The Cubs missed the playoffs. Still, everyone was pretty sure Garciaparra would be his usual, stellar self in 2005. Instead, he collapsed with a torn groin three weeks into the season. He was only hitting .157 at the time. He played a grand total of 62 games in 2005, finishing with a flurry to bring his batting average up to a modest .283. The ultimate kicker would come in 2006, when he returned to form and had an outstanding season...for the Los Angeles Dodgers.

82. Cubs Unveil '80s Night (2005)

It was bad enough the Cubs' marketing department decided to foist '70s Night on Chicago fans in 1996. Adding an '80s version a few years later was just plain offensive. It would be different if the franchise actually had any decent memories from the decade. But as it stands, all '80s Night did was remind every Cubs fan that not only did the team compile a 735–821 record during that time period (plus two October choke jobs), but we were all wearing the dumbest fashions ever concocted while we watched them do it. From the tight-rolled, stonewashed jeans to the ripped, off-the-shoulder shirts, it was a fashion nightmare. And that doesn't even take into account the hair: bangs for the ladies and mullets for the men. But in yet another case of the Cubs not caring about their increasing cheese factor, they went ahead with the promo anyway. So instead of a washed-up actor singing the seventh-inning stretch, this particular night was commemorated by a washed-up '80s personality like Debbie "now call me Deborah" Gibson doing the honors, while everybody reminisced about how great the 1985 Chicago Bears were.

83. Cubs Unveil '70s Night (1996)

As if Cubs fans needed another reason to feel embarrassed about supporting a team that hasn't won a championship since 1908. Now they're supposed to do it wearing bell-bottoms and a fake Afro. One can just imagine what's going on in the minds of the random WGN viewer when he sees 40,000 people dressed like Disco Stu doing the cell-phone wave as the hapless Cubs drop another one, 10–2. The front office says it's all about fun at the ballpark, but you almost get the feeling they're just trying to come up with ways to distract fans from what's happening on the field. Don't watch another Cubs pitching phenom blow out his elbow! Instead, check out the chick next to you in the halter top and hot pants! Hot pants! And no '70s Night would be complete without 20 or 25 renditions of "YMCA" blasting over the loudspeakers while fans try to remember if the Cubs made the playoffs in the 1970s. Upon realizing the team didn't, however, the fans will simply shrug and order another 2000s-priced beer.

84. *Andre Dawson Hit in Head by Eric Show (1987)*

Andre Dawson went through many hot streaks in 1987 en route to winning the National League MVP Award, but "the Hawk" was never hotter than he was moments before San Diego Padres pitcher Eric Show hit him in the face with a fastball on July 7, 1987. The plunking came after Dawson had homered in three of his last five plate appearances, and it was pretty obvious to everyone involved that Show had beaned him on purpose. While Dawson lay on the ground, dazed and bleeding from a cut that would eventually require 24 stitches, his teammates picked fights all over the field. Eric Show had to be removed from the stadium for his own safety. The fans were angry and scared, and many were positive that this was another "Cubs moment" unfolding: surely Dawson's season would be over. Surprisingly, and uniquely, a moment of frustration and fear turned into a good thing for the North Siders as a young Greg Maddux proved his mettle by nailing Benito Santiago in the ribs in the next inning. Dawson returned to the lineup in short order, finishing the season with a career-high 49 home runs and his first and only Most Valuable Player Award.

85. Sammy Sosa Leaves Game Early (2004)

There was a time when Sammy Sosa was treated like a king in Chicago. That time was not 2004, when an aging, broken-down Sosa was on the outs with Cubs brass as well as Cub Nation. The decline had been steady and punctuated by events like the corked bat incident in 2003, the sneeze incident in 2004 (he allegedly had to go on the disabled list because of a "violent sneeze"), and the growing steroid rumors. Coupled with the fact that Sosa's numbers had fallen dramatically—he would finish the season with his lowest home run and RBI totals in over a decade—and everything finally came to a head on the last day of the season, when Sosa walked out on the team before the game was over. The Sammy Sosa era was officially over in Chicago, as the once-proud Cub would end his career with a pathetic 2005 season in Baltimore (14 HR, .221 average). The man who looked to replace Ernie Banks as Mr. Cub had become the goat of Chicago, an impressive feat considering the outlandish, record-breaking stats he compiled in 13 seasons at Wrigley Field. To this day, he remains the only major league player to hit more than 60 home runs three separate times. He's also the only Cub with more than 500 career home runs who nobody likes.

86. Sammy Sosa "No Speak English" at Steroid Hearings (2005)

Technically, he was a Baltimore Oriole at the time, but that didn't make things any better when Sammy Sosa was subpoenaed to appear before a senate judiciary committee in March 2005 to discuss the problem of steroids in sports.

Everyone knew Sammy as a Cub. And thanks to all the focus on steroids over the past two years, everyone assumed Sammy was on the juice when he broke all those records. Just like Mark McGwire. Just like Barry Bonds. But nobody expected Sosa to claim "he no speak English" as his defense. The guy spent his entire major league career extolling his own virtues as a "gladiator" during press interviews. No English? That's all the slugger had to say for himself? It was embarrassing enough for baseball, let alone the people of Chicago. The only saving grace came when he was out-embarrassed by McGwire, who repeatedly "refused to talk about the past," and Rafael Palmeiro, who denied ever using steroids...then failed a drug test a few months later. For Sosa, the hearings would prove to be the final nail in the coffin of his legacy as a Cub. Even if he makes it to the Hall of Fame—and that's a big "if" these days—the Cubs likely wouldn't even want to claim him.

87. Steve Goodman Releases "A Dying Cub Fan's Last Request" (1983)

How do you know your team might be doomed? Probably when people write entire songs about its futility, as was the case with folk singer and longtime Cubs fan Steve Goodman. Here's how WGN radio man Roy Leonard described Goodman's unveiling of the song on his program: "The most memorable of all the visits, however, occurred on March 16, 1983, when Steve [Goodman] and Jethro Burns walked into our WGN studios around 11:00 AM. They had just finished a weekend at Park West, and Steve said he had introduced a song the night before that he would like to sing on the radio for the first time. With Jethro on mandolin and Steve's guitar for accompaniment, 'A Dying Cub Fan's Last Request' was heard on the radio the first time. Little did we know." Nearly six minutes in length, the song tells the tale of a dying Cubs fan and his feelings about the team in general. The most famous stanza goes like this:

> Do they still play the blues in Chicago
> When baseball season rolls around?
> When the snow melts away
> Do the Cubbies still play
> In their ivy-covered burial ground?
> When I was a boy they were my pride and joy
> But now they only bring fatigue
> To the home of the brave
> The land of the free
> And the doormat of the National League.

88. Cubs Lose to New York Yankees in World Series (1938)

Losers of five straight World Series appearances, the Chicago Cubs successfully made it a six-pack in 1938 against the formidable New York Yankees. Swept 4–0 and outscored 22–9 in the Series, the Cubs were no match for the likes of Lou Gehrig, Joe DiMaggio, and the rest of the Bronx Bombers. Even Dizzy Dean and Bill "Spaceman" Lee couldn't help the Cubs scratch out a lone face-saving victory, as the two hurlers went a combined 0–3. On the bright side, the 1938 Chicago Cubs did make plenty of history, helping the

Yankees set multiple postseason records: New York catcher Bill Dickey tied a World Series record with four hits in one game; pitcher Lefty Gomez won his sixth straight World Series start; and the Yankees became the first team ever to win three consecutive World Series titles.

89. Hawk Harrelson's Vocabulary

How can another team's broadcaster frustrate Cubs fans so much? For starters, Ken "Hawk" Harrelson works in the same city. As the White Sox's color commentator, Harrelson and his many catchphrases reflect poorly on all Chicagoans. He also appears on local television 162 times per season, which means Cubs fans are subjected to terms like *ducksnort* and *can of corn* much too often. Other regrettable Harrelson sayings include: Texas-leaguer; grab some bench; Hiney Bird; I tell you what; mercy; he gone; chopper two hopper; rack 'em up; stretch; hang wiff'em; zone 'em in, reel 'em in, and light her up; sacks packed; time to cinch it up and hunker down; that one had eyes on it; that'll get the job done; down to the last bullet; ball-four base hit; and you can put it on the boards, yes.

Harrelson is also as much of a homer as you can get. His favorite pastime is criticizing umpires about their strike zones, claiming, "There have been two different zones today, one for them and one for us."

90. Cubs Ballgirl Marla Collins Fired for Posing in Playboy (1986)

Thanks to Marla Collins, the attractive Cubs ballgirl, the franchise actually had something decent to look at on the field in 1986. God knows it wasn't the baseball, as the Cubs would finish the season 20 games under .500 at 70–90. Instead, it was Collins's short shorts. But in July, perhaps on a whim, Collins decided to lose the familiar striped uniform and pose nude in *Playboy*. The photos didn't actually appear in the men's magazine until the September issue, but Cubs brass decided to fire Collins immediately upon learning of the pictures in late July. The real losers were the fans, who were forced to watch game action for the duration of the season. The pictures, meanwhile, turned out just fine, especially the one that featured Harry Caray pointing to a tattoo on Collins's exposed thigh. Caray was not fired.

91. Home Opener Snowed Out (2003)

Opening Day is supposed to be about hope, new beginnings, and the promise of a successful season. Such was the case in 2003, when three-time National League Manager of the Year Dusty Baker was set to manage his first home game with the Chicago Cubs. That's when Baker and Cub Nation were reminded who was really in charge in Chicago: the weather. Amazingly, the April 7 opener against the Montreal Expos was postponed because of snow. Not rain or sleet, but the white stuff. It was also plenty cold. Fans who had taken the day off to see their Cubs start a new era were instead treated to nothing but hassle. While the home portion of the season began on Tuesday, April 8, most ticket holders were unable to skip two days of work in a row. On the upside, the Cubs defeated the Expos 6–1 to bring their record to 4–3. On the downside, we all know how 2003 turned out.

92. Ronnie Woo Woo's Voice

It's somewhat novel the first time you hear it, but after 10 consecutive minutes this shriek-ish cheer makes you want to tear your own ears off: "Cubs woo! Cubs woo!" Or "Moises woo! Moises woo!" Or the ever-popular "Beer woo! Beer woo!" You get the idea. For decades, Ronnie "Woo Woo" Wickers has roamed Wrigley Field, supporting the Chicago Cubs with his trademark shriek. If you attend only one game a year, it probably won't bother you much. But for regular fans, especially those who frequent the bleachers, where Wickers spends most of his time, the act tires quickly. Despite his claim of being the biggest Cubs fan in the world—his stated goal is to be the team's unofficial mascot—Wickers is more of a nuisance than anything. Dressed in his dingy Cubs uniform, he loves being the center of attention, whether it's at Wrigley, in Arizona during spring training, at the Cubs Convention, or dancing with some drunken chick at a Wrigleyville bar. That's what's so frustrating about Wickers: he claims to be doing it all for the glory of the Cubs, but he spends most of his time drawing attention to himself. And then after the game he goes from bar to bar asking for "donations," in the form of money, food, or help with his electric bill.

93. Bruce Sutter Wins World Series—with Cardinals (1982)

It's always a bittersweet moment when an ex-Cub wins the World Series with another team. Bruce Sutter's championship in 1982 was especially tough on the North Side, as it came just two years after the Cubs traded Sutter to division rival St. Louis. The future Hall of Famer began his career with the Cubs in 1976. Over the next five seasons, he compiled a stellar 2.39 ERA, saving 133 games. He went to four All-Star Games as a Cub and even won the Cy Young Award in 1979. Apparently, all this success wasn't what the Cubs looked for in a reliever, so they decided to trade Sutter to the Cardinals after the 1980 season. To nobody's surprise, Sutter flourished in St. Louis, winning the World Series his second year with the Cards and saving a career-high 45 games in 1984. Because he was in the same division as the Cubs, he also spent a great deal of his time stymieing Chicago hitters. Sutter was inducted into the Hall of Fame in 2006—as a Cardinal.

94. Cubs Acquire Jeromy Burnitz (2005)

Sammy Sosa was finally gone. After an amazing Cubs career, Sosa had worn out his welcome over the previous few summers, so Wrigleyville was more than happy to see the aging slugger leave for Baltimore. But...Jeromy Burnitz? That's who the Cubs chose to carry on the legacy of Andre Dawson and Sammy Sosa in right field? In the pantheon of disappointing Cubs signings, it wasn't quite Todd Hundley bad, but it was not much better. Burnitz was coming off a decent offensive season in Colorado. Which means the 30+ homers and 100+ RBIs totals were essentially meaningless. Freddie Bynum could hit 30 home runs in the thin air of Colorado. Burnitz also had a track record of striking out at an alarming pace, to the tune of a strikeout every other at-bat...or at least that's what it felt like. Overall, he wasn't nearly the offensive threat Cubs fans were looking for, especially considering that the team had also let Moises Alou go after the 2004 season. With such a big hole in the lineup, Burnitz had no chance to fill it. When he hit just .253 with 24 home runs and 87 RBIs in 2005, nobody was surprised.

95. Cubs Lose to Philadelphia Athletics in World Series (1929)

Joe McCarthy managed the North Siders to a 98–54 record, but the franchise would lose for the third time in its last three World Series appearances. By now fans were starting to get restless. It didn't help that 1929 also kicked off the Great Depression, so Cubs fans were unhappy in more ways than one. But while the Depression would fizzle out by the end of the 1930s, the Cubs' woes would only worsen.

In this particular Series, the problem was a lack of clutch hitting. Hack Wilson, who drove in 159 runs during the regular season—and just one year later would set a single-season record of 191 RBIs—had a grand total of 0 RBIs in five games. Rogers Hornsby batted .381 during the season, but just .238 in the World Series. At least he drove in more runs than Wilson, although it would be more accurate to say "run," as he only knocked in one. The lowest point came in Game 4, when the Cubs led 8–0 going into the bottom of the seventh inning. The Athletics scored 10 runs in the frame and eventually won the game 10–8, marking the biggest rally in World Series history. The Cubs had a chance to get out of the inning, but it was kept alive when star outfielder Hack Wilson misplayed a fly ball into a three-run, inside-the-park home run. Reportedly, this was the first time a fan said, "Only the Cubs" after a comically bad play. It would not be the last.

96. A.J. Pierzynski Hits Game-Winning Home Run (2006)

Any other team and it would have just been a tough loss. Any other hitter and it would have just been a game-winning homer. But it wasn't just any other team or any other hitter on Saturday, July 1, 2006. It was A.J. Pierzynski of the Chicago White Sox. Less than two months after brawling with Cubs catcher Michael Barrett after running him over at home plate, Pierzynski hit a 1–1 Ryan Dempster pitch into Wrigley's right-field bleachers for a three-run homer to erase a one-run deficit. The blast gave the White Sox an 8–6 victory over the poor Cubs, but that's not all it gave the South Siders. It gave them bragging rights all over again: The very player who incited the brawl was needling the Cubs once more, only this time with his bat. It was bad enough that Sox fans were saying Pierzynski took Barrett's sucker punch with ease, but now their guy was taunting North Siders with his bat, too.

97. Jimmy Buffett Plays Wrigley Field (2005)

According to Amazon.com, sellers of the *Jimmy Buffet Live at Wrigley Field* DVD, "Wrigleyville was transformed into Margaritaville as Jimmy Buffett, his band, and many thousands of his dancing, beer-guzzling, Hawaiian shirt–wearing, lei-draped fans invaded the venerable Chicago baseball stadium over Labor Day weekend, 2005." We couldn't have

Jimmy Buffett's party at Wrigley Field hasn't done anything in the way of improving the Cubs' bullpen woes.

said it better ourselves, but just for kicks, we'll try: lame. So very lame. When the Cubs first announced they would start holding concerts at Wrigley Field, it was a rather exciting new revenue source. Sure, the money wouldn't go to fielding a better team, but at least the Tribune would benefit. Adding insult to injury, the Cubs gave first concert rights to Jimmy Buffett and his merry band of cheeseballs. So while the Cubs were off playing their way to a fourth-place finish, 40-year-old drunk dudes in coconut bras and grass skirts were soiling hallowed Wrigley Field. Once again, the Cubs had given die-hard fans a cornucopia of reasons to be ashamed of their favorite franchise.

98. Alex Gonzalez Fumbles Easy Grounder After Bartman Play (2003)

Everybody wants to blame poor Steve Bartman for the 2003 Cubs playoff collapse. Or, if they actually decide to point fingers at someone on the field, they choose Mark Prior, who quickly disintegrated in the eighth inning of Game 6 of the NLCS against the Florida Marlins. The guy nobody seems to remember is Cubs shortstop Alex Gonzalez. While the Bartman Incident set the scene, the rally didn't officially get out of hand until a few batters later. With the Cubs up 3–0, Marlins catcher Ivan Rodriguez singled to make the score 3–1. There was still no inkling of what was to come, especially when the batter after Rodriguez, Miguel Cabrera, hit a tailor-made double-play ball to Gonzalez at short. Unfortunately for Cub Nation, the normally sure-handed Gonzalez muffed the grounder. So instead of ending the half-inning by turning two, the Cubs let the door swing wide open—and the Marlins scored seven more runs. By the time the final out of the frame was recorded, the Marlins led 8–3 and were on their way to one of the most improbable turnarounds in NLCS history. Gonzalez was shipped to the Montreal Expos in 2004 as part of the four-team trade that brought his replacement, Nomar Garciaparra, to the Cubs.

99. Richard Marx Appears in Cubs Uniform in "Take This Heart" Music Video (1991)

There are so many things wrong with this particular Richard Marx music video; it's difficult to know where to begin. The hair? The lyrics? The horrible cinematography? In what might be one of the most confusing entertainment creations of all time, the video can best be described like this: Hall of Fame broadcaster Bob Uecker narrates the action as second-rate pop star Richard Marx hits a World

Series–winning home run for the Chicago Cubs off Oakland Athletics closer Dennis Eckersley while a variety of major league players and coaches look on, including Greg Maddux, Tony La Russa, Jose Canseco, and Rickey Henderson, the last of whom fails to catch the ball despite a high-flying leap above the outfield wall. Between pitches, Marx and his longhaired bandmates do a rockin' version of "Take This Heart" all over an empty baseball stadium. Sometimes they're on the field, sometimes they're in the stands, sometimes we see the crew filming them, and sometimes we even flash back to see Marx training with the Cubs throughout the season. After the girlish pop star finally delivers the historic home run for the Cubs, despite an 0–2 count and a hopelessly awkward swing, he wakes up to discover it was all a dream! In a word: abomination.

100. Cubs Tagged as "Lovable Losers" (Post-1945)

When a franchise becomes so synonymous with losing that people feel the need to put a positive spin on it, that's frustrating. It also doesn't strike much fear in the hearts of other teams. "Hey Albert," St. Louis Cardinals manager Tony La Russa might say. "You think we'll be able to take two of three from, let's see here, the Lovable Losers? Oh, my mistake. I didn't realize we were playing the Cubs. This should be a walk in the park." The worst part about the nickname is that it suggests losing is okay as long as you're affable. The Tribune Company has latched on to this idea, worrying more about the "brand image" of the ballclub than the quality of the team on the field.

APPENDIX C

Frequently Asked Questions

Q: Am I supposed to take this guide seriously?
A: Yes. Too many self-help books are filled with small-minded theories about how to enhance your self-esteem or maximize your potential. Those books are difficult to follow and almost never result in an improved you. This guide is all about making yourself feel better no matter what life throws your way. It provides simple ways to deal with adversity and features easy-to-apply tactics such as "drink more beer" and "just don't worry about it."

Q: A lot of people make fun of Cubs fans. Will my friends mock me for reading this book?
A: They might, yes.

Q: I'm a New York Yankees fan. Will this book work for me?
A: It will probably work even better for you. Imagine you've taken chapter 1 to heart. Just when you're about to wait for Next Year, you realize your club is going to the playoffs this year. That makes this season that much sweeter. The same can be said for the other principles,

from the Power of Low Expectations to Beer Will Make It Better!™ Because in case you were wondering, yes, beer will also make winning better.

Q: Wouldn't it be easier for Cubs fans to just root for another team? In other words, aren't these people asking for trouble?
A: So you want them to give up? What are you, some sort of communist? America was founded on the ideals of perseverance and struggle. What if Ben Franklin or George Clooney had simply given up? Not only would you be reading this sentence by candlelight, we'd all be without one of Hollywood's most likeable leading men. Asking Cubs fans to switch their allegiance is like asking an American to root for France in the Olympics just because France has a better soccer team. It's not going to happen. And it shouldn't!

Q: Most of your practical applications seem to be geared toward men. Is that because this guide is more useful for males than for females?
A: Not at all. I'm just too lazy to think of unisexual examples. Hell, I'm too lazy to check if *unisexual* is even a word.

Q: What's the best postgame bar in Wrigleyville?
A: Man, that's tough, because every one of them sells beer. But I would have to go with Gingerman Tavern on Clark and Grace. The Full Shilling is pretty good, too. Steer clear of John Barleycorn's unless you're a meathead.

The 2003 Ford Taurus is the ideal vehicle for any Cubs fan.

Q: I'm thinking of getting a new car. What kind of car would a Cubs fan buy?

A: That's a great question. By patterning your purchasing habits after Cubs fans, you can really get inside their heads. As for the specific make and model, it's obvious: a 2003 Ford Taurus. It's all-American, not flashy, and you don't have to worry about it getting your hopes up. Okay, this car might be kinda ugly. It might even break down every once in a while, but most of the time it'll run just fine. And Cubs fans have always been comfortable with "just fine," so you should be, too.

Q: Since we're on the subject, what brand of clothing should I wear?

A: Well, you're gonna want something that will make you happy. Cubs fans usually wear Derrek Lee jerseys. That might not be appropriate in every situation, however, so you'll need a steady supply of Old Navy items.

Q: Who are some famous Cubs fans? Do they agree with the assertions in this book?

A: Noteworthy Cubs fans include Bill Murray, John Cusack, William Petersen, Bonnie Hunt, Jim Belushi, George Will, Joe Mantegna, Vince Vaughn, and Gary Sinise. As of August 25, 2006, all of these people subscribe to this book's theories, maybe, if you were to ask them.

Q: What do Cubs fans do in the off-season?

A: That's the beauty of being a Cubs fan. There really isn't an off-season in the traditional sense. Cubs faithful find all kinds of ways to make rooting for their team a year-long process. If you're referring to the months between October and March, Cubs fans are typically busy during this time of year. From decompressing after the season in November and December to the Cubs Convention in January, to the start of spring training in February, these people are always thinking Cubs. It's also a great time to earn extra money so you can afford tickets for next season.

Q: I've never been to Wrigley Field. Where are the best seats in the stadium?

A: The left-field bleachers. On the flip side, the worst place to sit is right behind one of those steel girders holding up the upper deck. You can't see anything, and the friend you brought to the game will hate you all day.

Q: Is it ever appropriate to do "the wave" at Wrigley Field?
A: Sure. If you're a loser. Or if it's suddenly 1988.

Q: What would happen if I lived my life like a White Sox fan?
A: Initially, it might feel good to not worry about showering, shaving, or abiding by the laws of our country, but eventually, you'd probably end up lonely and incarcerated.

Q: You say that "Beer Will Make It Better!™" But how do I know how much beer it will take?
A: It's a long process of trial and error, but it's a fun one. A good rule of thumb is if you can stand on one foot, you haven't had enough. If you don't remember your name, you've had too much.

Beer Will Make It Better!™, but you have to know when you've had too much.

Q: Is it true you founded *The Heckler?*

A: Yes, I cofounded the satirical Chicago sports newspaper known as *The Heckler* with my friend Brad Zibung. Brad is a lot more responsible than I am, so his title is editor in chief, while I am relegated to being second in command with a pathetic title of managing editor. I'm funnier, though, as anyone who knows both of us will tell you. I'm also more of an idea man, while he just talks on the phone and pushes papers around. Before we started *The Heckler*, Brad and I worked together on RightFieldSucks.com.

Q: Where can I find hard copies of *The Heckler?*

A: In addition to the blue honor boxes strategically positioned throughout Chicago, *The Heckler* is available at hundreds of bars and restaurants. You can even have the paper delivered right to your door by subscribing online at www.theheckler.com.

Cubs Fan's Glossary

Alley: Urinal

Bad luck: The reason Cubs fans believe their team hasn't won a World Series in nearly 100 years

Beer goggles: Those things that make every girl at Sports Corner totally sexy, even the one who turns out to be a guy

Blanco'd: Term used in the unlikely event backup catcher Henry Blanco drives in a run (i.e., You've been Blanco'd!)

Bleacher bum: A bleacher season ticket holder or a drunk college kid who thinks swearing is the same as heckling

Bud Light Bleachers: The largest singles bar in the country

Bullpen: Part of Wrigley Field that houses Cubs players who should still be in the minor leagues

Bush-league: Style of play often associated with Chicago's North Side franchise

Catcher's interference: When Cubs catcher Michael Barrett's inability to call a good game interferes with the Cubs winning

Cash cow: The Tribune Company's pet name for the Cubs

Clubhouse: Where the Cubs go to lick their wounds after being shut out, again

Coffers: Where the Tribune Company keeps the overwhelming profits made from the Cubs

Crazy: Mental state of people willing to spend $60 on bleacher tickets for a Tuesday-night game against the Pittsburgh Pirates

Day-to-day: Catchall phrase used to describe how often the prognosis can change for Mark Prior's most recent injury

Disabled list: Where 50 percent of Cubs players will spend any given season

Double play: What the Cubs hit into with one man out and the tying run at third in the bottom of the ninth

Doubleheader: A rare chance for the Cubs to lose two games in one day

Eamus catuli: A rooftop phrase used to confuse Cubs fans

Elbow: Ironically, a Cubs pitcher's Achilles Heel

ERA: How long it has been since the North Siders won a World Series...an entire era

Error: A mistake (i.e., Cubs GM Jim Hendry made an error when he traded away pitching prospect Dontrelle Willis)

Fielder's choice: A Cubs hitter's version of an infield hit

Fork: What can usually be stuck in the Cubs around mid-July, as they are most likely done for the season

Friendly Confines: Wrigley Field's nickname, which arose shortly after the stadium's completion, when opposing teams realized how easy it was to win there

Front office: Part of the Cubs organization responsible for explaining away latest price increases

Grand slam: Daryle Ward's favorite breakfast order

Happiness: An elusive state of well-being, if you're a Cubs fan

Heckler, The: A satirical Chicago sports publication known for being totally awesome and really funny

Hey, Hey!: Exclamation uttered by drunken bleacher fans when a tight-shirted female is spotted nearby

Hi-Tops: Last-resort meeting place for fans who didn't find someone to hook up with during the game

Holy cow!: Harry Caray's famous catchphrase—or one of those big fat nuns who attends the day games

Home run: What most Cubs players try to achieve with women after the game

Hope: A belief that things will get better, not worse, which is way more possible

Hustle: A characteristic Aramis Ramirez has not displayed once in his entire career

Hype: Misguided excitement that often surrounds the Cubs' minor league prospects

If: A pivotal word in the vocabulary of Cubs fans. Through *if* all things are possible, including overcoming a five-game deficit in the standings with only six games left to play.

Injury: What Mark Prior suffers every five or six weeks

Ivy: One of those "intangibles" that brings people to the park despite all the losses

Jail: Common hangout for many Chicago White Sox fans

Kangaroo court: Ad hoc committee that fines Cubs players for doing things right

Lose: What the Cubs usually do when they play other teams

Mai tai: Overpriced alcoholic beverage used to "make self feel better about hooking up again this weekend"

Next Year: When the Cubs are rumored to win the World Series

Optimism: Thinking the Cubs won't get swept this weekend

Pop out: What a Cubs hitter is good for with two outs and the bases loaded

Proud partner: What the Cubs call a company that gives them overwhelming amounts of cash to splash its logo somewhere inside the stadium

Rally: Scoring a flurry of runs in a short span of time to erase a deficit. The Cubs are great at almost doing this.

Reliever: For the Cubs, this is typically a pitcher with a 5.00+ ERA

Sacrifice: When a Cubs player takes one for the team after the game at John Barleycorn's

Scalp: The part of a male Cubs fan's head that hair falls out of as a result of yet another one-run Cubs loss

Scapegoat: Cause of every problem to ever encounter any Cubs fan

Screwball: Cubs ace Carlos Zambrano

Single: The kind of women former Cub Kyle Farnsworth loves to get his hands on—though he'll take "Married" or "Any" as well

Skybox: Gathering place for "friends of the Cubs" and other rich people

Slump: What a Cubs hitter goes through from April to June, when the games actually matter

Streak: Two Cubs wins in a row

Strikeout: The outcome of a typical Cubs player's at-bat

Strike zone: An area above the plate Cubs pitchers usually have trouble finding

Talent: A trait rarely found in the Cubs' minor league prospects

Triple: The kind of cheeseburger Carlos Zambrano prefers at Wendy's

Umpire: Who Cubs pitchers tend to blame when things don't go their way

Urinal: Alley

Walk: The outcome of one out of every 1,000 Corey Patterson at-bats as a Cub

Walk of shame: Refers to how Cubs players exit the field after the end of a typical game

Wave, the: Ballpark activity that should have ended in 1994

WGN: We Got Nothing

Win: What the other team usually does when they play the Cubs at Wrigley

Wrigleyville: Beer drinker's paradise

Wrigleyville Premium Ticket Services: "Legal" scalping operation owned and run by the Chicago Cubs